THE BERKSHIRE TRAVELLER

ALMANACK
& JOURNAL

ALSO FROM THE BERKSHIRE TRAVELLER PRESS:

Country Inns & Back Roads
The Indian In Connecticut
True Stories of Old New England — Yankees All
Once Told Tales of Old New England
Shop Drawings of Shaker Furniture and Woodenware
The Berkshire Traveller Resort Book
The Boy With The Sun Tree Bow
Treasured Recipes of Country Inns

FORTHCOMING:

First Encounter: The Indian
in Massachusetts and Rhode Island
Stockbridge: 1739 — 1973
The Berkshire Traveller Book of Cities

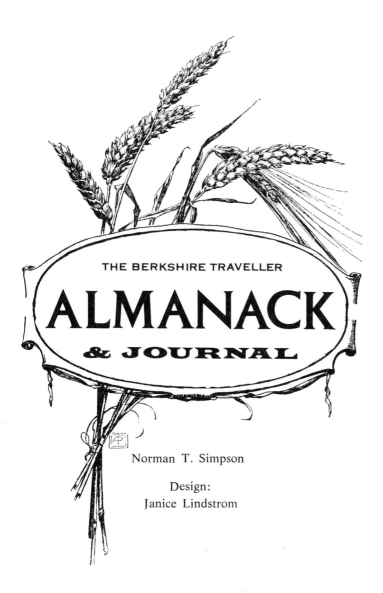

THE BERKSHIRE TRAVELLER

ALMANACK

& JOURNAL

Norman T. Simpson

Design:
Janice Lindstrom

THE BERKSHIRE TRAVELLER PRESS
Stockbridge, Massachusetts 01262

Shaker recipes courtesy of:
Pleasant Hill, Shakertown, Kentucky.

Cover Painting:
THE QUILTING PARTY
Oil on Wood, 1840-1850.
Courtesy of Rockefeller Collection
Williamsburg, Virginia

ISBN No. 0-912944-06-4
Library of Congress Card Number 73-83795
Copyright 1973   The Berkshire Traveller Press

Well, Hello once again —

This is the second time that we've gotten together, although it's quite by chance that it's about a year since our previous meeting. This time we've added the word *Journal* to the title as there seem to be quite a few personal reminiscences included.

While dictionaries vary somewhat in their definitions of an almanack, we prefer to think of this book as being a group of favorite aphorisms, poems, epigrams and quotations. We've also included more helpful observations and seasonal hints about bird and plant life, the weather and some disconcerting if not useful trivia. It may or may not be written anew each year.

A portion of this offering was compiled as a diversion while traveling, writing, editing and publishing "Country Inns & Back Roads." The first drafts were hastily scribbled on the backs of envelopes, unpaid bills, timetables and menus in various parts of the United States, Canada and England.

The remainder unfolded in the snug library of my Berkshire farmhouse where there is a wealth of old books, maps and albums of family photographs from which to draw poignant memories.

The Berkshire Traveller

JANUARY

The month of January was named for Janus (meaning "door"), the two-faced Roman god of beginnings. With one face looking back over the past and one looking ahead to the future, Janus' month was appropriately assigned the position of the first month of the year, after being the eleventh month for many years on the early Roman calendar. On January 1, 153 B.C., the day the new consuls took office, January became the start of the Roman civil year.

For all of its "beginnings," on the American Football calendar, strangely enough, January marks the end of a very exciting and exhausting football season.

BIRDS

Chickadees, grosbeaks, crossbills, cardinals, towhees, cedar wax-wings and woodpeckers winter in New England. One may also spot a vagrant rough-legged hawk seeking its prey, or a kingfisher feeding out of the open spots in fresh water. This is the best month to look for wintering owls such as the Saw-whet, Great Horned, Long-eared, and Barred owls. They are most frequently seen roosting in pine groves, although they are hard to distinguish from the dark branches.

FLOWERS

Winter jasmine, winter sweet, Christmas rose, and winter aconites have blossomed, and the creeping sweetbox blooms best after a deep snow. When the temperature falls below freezing the leaves of the rhododendron will curl as though shivering with cold. They hang tight and blacken if it drops below 20 degrees.

You can brighten your home indoors with bromeliads, double impatiens (needs sun), hanging baskets of episcia plants (needs moderate light), Jerusalem cherry (needs a cool but sunny place), and fairy primrose. For quick bloom, plant some paper white narcissus indoors in a bowl of pebbles and water. Flowering holiday plants will last longer if they are placed in a window where they will get good light but no direct sunlight. Keep a poinsettia in a consistently warm place and water it with warm water.

SHAKER DRIED APPLE CAKE

INGREDIENTS

1¾ cups flour, sifted	1 cup dried apples (or apricots)
2 teaspoons baking soda	1 cup molasses
1 teaspoon cinnamon	2/3 cup sour cream
½ teaspoon cloves	1 cup sugar
½ teaspoon salt	1 egg

DIRECTIONS

Soak dried apples overnight. In the morning cut fine and simmer in molasses for 20 minutes. Cool. Combine cream, sugar and egg and beat until smooth. Combine dry ingredients and sift several times. Blend both mixtures and beat until smooth. Add dry fruit and molasses. Turn into buttered loaf pan and bake in 350 degree oven for 1 hour. This is a very tasty dessert; the dried apples take on a citron flavor.

January 2

I was awakened one morning this week with a rat-a-tat-tat on my downstairs window which opens on to the bird feeder. At first I thought it was a lost traveler, as we enjoyed a six-inch snowfall during the night. Perhaps this was Archimedes or Aristophanes searching for an honest man. In any case, I put on my wool robe and went down, and there was a red-breasted nuthatch hanging upside down on my window pecking away on the glass to attract attention to the fact that the bird-feeder was empty. I've always thought of the nuthatch as being an insect eater, but I guess that any bird that travels head first down a tree is entitled to his own whims.

January 5

THE SNOW

It sifts from leaden sieves,
It powders all the wood,
It fills with alabaster wool
The wrinkles of the road.

It makes an even face
Of mountains and of plain,
Unbroken forehead from the east
Unto the east again.

It reaches to the fence,
It wraps it, rail by rail,
Till it is lost in fleeces;
It flings a crystal veil.

On stump and stack and stem,—
The summer's empty room,
Acres of seams where harvests were,
Recordless, but for them.

It ruffles wrists of posts,
As ankles of a queen,—
Then it stills its artisans like ghosts,
Denying they have been.
                                    EMILY DICKINSON

January 15

This is generally the week of The Discussion on Removing the Christmas Tree. It's been up since the week before Christmas and the needles are brown in spite of all the numerous attempts to keep water in the base. But I am reluctant to remove this reminder of Jesus' birth and the joy of the season. I am happy to say that there is a family in the village that keeps their outdoor Christmas tree lighted well into February. I think January needs a little cheer.

JANUARY 19

A sudden severe cold spell for two or three days this week caused me to wonder how in the world the winter birds could stand such severe weather, and culling a few books on birdlore I found it is a combination of energy-building food and the well nigh perfect insulation—a coat of feathers. There is no circulation in the feet, and the blood in the rest of the diminutive bodies circulates with tremendous speed. I understand that some chickadees' heartbeats are 600 beats per minute. This is one of the reasons they're always busy hunting for more food and in this season of the year I can open my window next to the feeder with my hand full of seed and have some of these wild creatures actually perch on my fingers and eat the seed from my palm. There is something beautiful and wonderful about it—this kind of trust between God's creatures.

Blow, blow, thou winter wind,
Thou art not so unkind
  As man's ingratitude;
Thy tooth is not so keen,
Because thou art not seen,
  Although thy breath be rude.
Heigh ho! sing, heigh ho! unto the green holly;
Most friendship is feigning, most loving mere folly:
  Then, heigh ho, the holly!
  This life is most jolly.

WILLIAM SHAKESPEARE

JANUARY 24

On January 24th 1848, gold was discovered in the valley of the Sacramento River in California, thereby setting off a chain reaction that is still going on. Men gave up ther jobs, left their wives, stole from their employers, mortgaged their farms, and almost sold their soul for the opportunity to get in on the big bonanza. Wouldn't you like to have the smallest possible grain of gold, the most minute speck of it, for every book, play, motion picture, and now—oh joy unbounded—television program based on the great madness. We would indeed all be as rich as Croesus.

JANUARY 25

I am reminded that on January 25, 1759, Bobby Burns came into this world:

O my luve is like a red, red rose
That's newly sprung in June.
O my luve is like the melodie,
That's sweetly played in tune.

As fair art thou, my bonnie lass,
So deep in luve am I,
And I will luve thee still, my dear,
Till a' the seas gang dry.

Till a' the seas gang dry, my dear,
And the rocks melt wi' the sun!
And I will luve thee still, my dear,
While the sands o' life shall run.
ROBERT BURNS

JANUARY 26

A lot of things and people emerged during Januarys of the past. The ill-fated League of Nations was established January 10, 1920, and the first U.N. General Assembly met on the same day 26 years later. John Hancock, who is spoken of as a great patriot but who is also sometimes referred to as a great opportunist, was born in January along with Robert E. Lee, General Douglas MacArthur and Franklin D. Roosevelt.

Wolfgang Mozart first saw the light of day in January, 1756. It would be interesting a thousand years from now to see which of these men has stood the test of time. Looking backward, there are a few generals that might come into memory: Alexander the Great, Julius Caesar, Attilla the Hun, Pancho Villa, the Duke of Wellington and maybe a handful more.

However, it speaks well for man's progress that creative spirits like Praxiteles, Myron, Homer, Aristophanes, Socrates, Terence, Jesus, Erasmus and thousands of others are doing much better.

JANUARY 27

For as the earth bringeth forth her bud, and as the garden causeth the things that are sown in it to spring forth; so the Lord God will cause righteousness and praise to spring forth before all the nations.

ISAIAH 61:11

SWEET DISORDER

A sweet disorder in the dress
Kindles in clothes a wantonness;
A lawn about the shoulders thrown
Into a fine distraction—
An erring lace, which here and there
Enthrals the crimson stomacher—
A cuff neglectful, and thereby
Ribbands to flow confusedly—
A winning wave, deserving note,
In the tempestuous petticoat—
A careless shoe-string, in whose tie
I see a wild civility—
Do more bewitch me than when art
Is too precise in every part.

ROBERT HERRICK

"Kindles in clothes a wantoness" is it? This week some good friends in the next village, inspired no doubt to relieve the chilly embrace of winter, invited a great many people to their rather large house to enjoy, of all things, a dance. Many came in their sedate gray and blue suits and the proper-length dancing gowns. However, the Younger Generation came in whatever Fancy directed, and wouldn't Robert Herrick have been deeply impressed with the neglected cuffs and the confused ribbands and the tempestuous petticoats! Although there were few enough of these since both genders seemed to favor flair-bottomed blue dungarees. Indeed, young Herrick would have been bewitched beyond belief with the lack of precision in every part.

Ben Franklin

Benjamin Franklin was born on January 17, 1706. If all the sayings attributed both correctly and incorrectly to "Poor Richard" were placed end to end they would probably reach from here to Philadelphia and be multiplying on the way. It's amazing how many of the aphorisims penned by "B. Franklin" or one of his scriveners have come to be continued in common usage today.

How few there are who have courage enough to own their Faults, or resolution enough to mend them!

No better relation than a prudent and faithful Friend.

Content makes poor Men rich; Discontent makes rich Men poor.

You can bear your own Faults, why not a Fault in your Wife?

Avarice and Happiness never saw each other, how then should they become acquainted?

He that would live in peace and at ease, must not speak all he knows, nor judge all he sees.

Who is rich? He that rejoices in his portion.

He that drinks his cyder alone, let him catch his horse alone.

Quarrels never could last long, If on one side only lay the wrong.

The King's cheese is half wasted in parings: but no matter, 'tis made of the People's milk.

Let all Men know thee, but no man know thee thoroughly: Men freely ford that see the shallows.

The way to see by Faith is to shut the Eye of Reason.

Hide not your Talents, they for Use were made: "What's a Sun-Dial in the Shade?"

The same man cannot be both Friend and Flatterer.

> *The poor have little,*
> *Beggars none;*
> *The rich too much*
> *Enough not one.*

Hear no ill of a Friend, nor speak any of an Enemy.

If you would keep your secret from an Enemy, tell it not to a Friend.

Beware of little Expenses: a small leak will sink a great Ship.

There are no ugly loves, nor handsome prisons.

Great talkers, little doers.

1. *The Skaters* by Peter Bruegel, the Elder (1525-1569)

This is the first of four plates we have included in this book which dramatically illustrates the tremendous talent of the Flemish master. Bruegel has been called the greatest 16th century Flemish master in the depiction of scenes from ordinary life.

C Cum gratia: vt pa-
tet in suis priuilegijs.

february

February was the twelfth month on the early Roman calendar. It was a month devoted to the anticipation of the new
year with its many ceremonies of purification and of the
cult of the dead. One such ceremony involved the sacrifice
of a goat, after which the priests walked around striking
the women on the back of the hands with a strip of goatskin,
thus insuring fertility and safe delivery. Its name derived
from februare, meaning "to purify."

According to ancient British weatherlore, the 12th, 13th, and 14th days indicated the weather for the remainder of the year: if it were stormy on those days, the year would be fair-weathered and vice-versa.

BIRDS:

Natural food is scarce at this time, so it is particularly important to keep the birdfeeders filled. This is a good time to clean out birdhouses and nesting boxes before the birds arrive from from their sojourn south. The birdhouses may also be dusted with a pyrethrin product to control lice.

In February, formations of Canada geese pass overhead on their way north to summer residence, and grackles return in flocks. One may also catch a glimpse of an early robin, bluebird, or redwing. At this time, colorful displays of male ducks set territory and perform peculiar courtship rites. Ducks are most commonly found along the Northeastern coastline, in sheltered coves and rivers, in ponds and streams, or in shallow inlets.

FLOWERS:

Azara, snowdrops and spring snowflakes add color and fragrance to bleak February days. Near the end of the month, the harbingers of Spring—crocus and skunk cabbage—will begin to push their way up, even beneath the snow.

It is a good time to start seeds indoors for peppers, tomatoes, eggplant, impatiens, and petunias. Although there are several different ways to start them (various kits can be purchased), the basic needs are adequate moisture, proper light (a sunny window or a 40 watt flourescent light) and temperature (usually room temperature), and sufficient nutrients. After sowing the seeds, cover the container with plastic to retain the moisture. Remove this cover as soon as the first seedlings break ground.

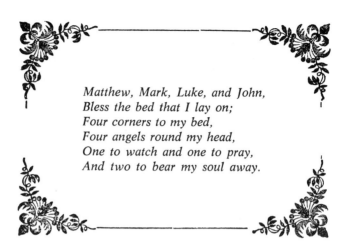

Matthew, Mark, Luke, and John,
Bless the bed that I lay on;
Four corners to my bed,
Four angels round my head,
One to watch and one to pray,
And two to bear my soul away.

FEBRUARY 3

I just took note of the fact that Charles Dickens was born on Friday, the second of February in 1812. It seems appropriate that he should have been born during the winter months because I, for one, always seemed to associate him with scenes that had snow on the ground. A poignant memory for me is W.C. Fields playing the role of Mr. Micawber in the cinema, "David Copperfield." I learned just recently that the model for the character was actually Dickens' father, a man constantly in debt and difficulty, for whom nothing "really turned up." Also, his mother was the original Mrs. Nicholas Nickleby.

Dickens visited America two times and stayed in famous hostelries of the mid-nineteenth century including the Golden Lamb in Lebanon, Ohio. It is very possible that no novelist was ever so popular in his own country in his own time.

Not everybody saw Dickens as the Great Hope of English letters. Oscar Wilde once said of him: "One must have a heart of stone to read the death of Little Nell without laughing."

"She was dead. No sleep so beautiful and calm, so free from trace of pain, so fair to look upon. She seemed a creature fresh from the hand of God, and waiting for the breath of life; not one who had lived and suffered death.

"Her couch was dressed with here and there some winter berries and green leaves, gathered in a spot she had been used to favor. "When I die, put near me something that has loved the light, and had the sky above it always." Those were her words.

"She was dead. Dear, gentle, patient, noble Nell, was dead. Her little bird—a poor, slight thing the pressure of a finger would have crushed—was stirring nimbly in its cage; and the strong heart of its child-mistress was mute and motionless for ever.

"Where were the traces of her early cares, her sufferings, and fatigues? All gone. Sorrow was dead indeed in her, but peace and perfect happiness were born; imaged in her tranquil beauty and profound repose.

"And still her former self lay there, unaltered in this change. Yes. The old fireside had smiled upon that same sweet face it had passed, like a dream, through haunts of misery and care, at the door of the poor schoolmaster on the summer evening, before the furnace fire upon the cold wet night, at the still bedside of the dying boy, there had been the same mild, lovely look. So shall we know the angels in their majesty, after death."

OLD CURIOSITY SHOP
Charles Dickens

However, Dickens was not the only one to feel the heavy acid of Wilde's pen. Wilde spoke of another Victorian: "Mr. Henry James writes fiction as if it were a painful duty."

FEBRUARY 11

What a great thing it is to awaken well past nine on the clock of a winter's morning and realize that you might have easily slept untill noon. Although I am an early riser and one who likes to greet the dawn of every day, it does give me a great satisfaction to oversleep. It's a secret vice.

"I have all my life long been lying 'til noon, yet I tell all young men and tell them with great sincerity, that nobody who does not rise early will ever do any good."

SAMUEL JOHNSON

HOURS OF SLEEP
Nature needs five; Custom takes seven
Laziness takes nine; And wickedness eleven.

FEBRUARY 14

This is the week in which Lincoln's birthday is celebrated, and I can recall a conversation with an elderly dealer in rare and antique books in which he elaborated on the fact that in

the first 50 years after Lincoln's assasination, there were more books written about him than about any other subject in the world's history.

It is also with some great sadness that I noted that on the 12th of February in 1554, Lady Jane Grey was beheaded.

> *When lovely woman stoops to folly,*
> *And finds too late that men betray,*
> *Which arm can soothe her melancholy?*
> *What art can wash her guilt away?*
> OLIVER GOLDSMITH

FEBRUARY 18

On this day there occurred an incident that rocked me to the very foundations of my convictions. I discovered that the American Heritage Dictionary of the English Language had no reference to that intrepid soldier, adventurer and literary figure, Miles Standish. It was on the 18 of February in 1621 that Miles Standish was named military leader of Plymouth Colony—as earth-shaking a piece of trivia that has ever been recorded. Tradition says that Miles was brave and valiant on the field of battle but he's best remembered for the fact that he was unable to press his courtship of the fair Priscilla who it develops, may have been the first women's-libber on our shores, as she encouraged John Alden to do his own thing.

FEBRUARY 22

Father, I cannot tell a lie, I did it with my little hatchet.

MARK TWAIN
Mark Twain as Washington

FEBRUARY 23

Where would we all be without Samuel Pepys, the great 17th century diarist who was born on February 23, 1623. In the first place, we wouldn't be rhyming his name with "steps" instead of "peeps," and maybe the world would be a better place. Secondly, all of the latter-day diarists would not have said at some time writing their tomes: "Up betimes."

Here are some excerpts from Mr. Pepys diary:

"I send my wife up to her closet to examine her kitchen accounts, and then I took occasion to fall out with her for buying a laced handkerchief and pinner without my leave. From this we both began to be angry and so continued 'til bed.

Sometime later: (Not related to above entry.)

"Waking this morning out of my sleep on a sudden, I did with my elbow hit my wife a great blow over her face and neck which waked her with pain which I was sorry, and to sleep again."

Still another:

"To the Strand, to my bookseller's, and there bought an idle roguish French book, which I had bought in plain binding avoiding the buying of it better bound, because I resolve, as soon as I have read it, to burn it, that it may not stand in the list of books, nor among them, to disgrace them if it should be found."

And thus we have mention of the first plain brown paper wrapping.

FEBRUARY 28

I'm always somewhat awed by the list of people and events that are associated with February. Besides St. Valentine, there is Babe Ruth, Adlai Stevenson, Thomas Edison, Abraham Lincoln, George Washington, John Glenn, Henry Wadsworth Longfellow, James Joyce, Victor Hugo and Charles Lamb.

I would also like to meet the guy who first thought up the Groundhog Day legend because it gets more publicity and press for nothing than any other event I can think of.

Oh yes, I also noted that the Boy Scouts of America were founded in 1910, thereby putting upon all of us the burden of doing one good deed a day or losing our merit badges.

Mackerel Skies & Running Sparks

There is probably more weather lore in the country regions than anywhere else. Since knowledge of weather is essential to farmers to harvest their crops successfully—and, since a slight miscalculation of the weather may well mean the difference (not between success and failure) but life and death to the fisherman, one can see how absolutely necessary it is for the countryman to be able to predict weather accurately.

You've heard—"Colder the night when the stars shine bright" . . . and "Rain before seven, clear before eleven." There are several other signs, especially to predict snow—a "bank" in the southwest being the best. Running sparks in the chimney is a sign of cold and a growling fire indicates snow and cold weather. "Squaw winter" (cold days in August) . . . wasps building high nests . . . the size of muskrat houses . . . the number of nuts gathered by squirrels . . . geese flying south . . . a dog lying behind a stove . . . whether a chicken's breastbone be white or dark . . . and the amount of melt in a hog . . . all are long-range signs to determine whether it will be a snowy or an "open" winter. Many of the signs for snow also apply to rain, depending on the season.

Northern lights predict a change in the weather. High tides . . . big seas . . . sun dogs . . . rings around the sun or moon . . . mare's tails . . . wind "backing against the sun," are all "weather breeders." When the spider "runs extra lines to his web," . . . when gulls fly inland . . . and when birds cease to cry—one can expect a storm.

One may look for snow in winter when the kettle boils dry . . . when smoke comes to the ground . . . or when flies infest the house. A cloud bank in the east at dawn . . . wind shifting with the sun . . . a clear sunset . . . or cobwebs in the morning all indicate fair weather—and, in the latter case, hot weather.

When the weather clears at night, it indicates that it will not stay clear long—but should it clear in the afternoon, the weather will stay clear for a "spell." Should you witness a mackerel sky . . . the sun setting in a bank of clouds or "setting double," or, if the wind is southeast . . . or if there is a mist on high hills early in the morning—look for snow.

For as long as man has been subject to the vicissitudes of weather, he has attempted to forecast it. Countrymen still forecast their own weather by a casual inspection of the state of the sky. On the basis of the sequence of weather events transpiring in their vicinities, some particularly keen observers make reasonably good predictions for the next 24 hours. In the northeastern part of our country they recognize that when the wind shifts into the east and clouds appear on the southwestern horizon, snow often follows within the next day. Meteorologists scoff . . . but the fact remains that a good weather-prophet . . . by employing the traditional signs and an intuitive sense . . . is correct far more often than one would normally expect. Those who frequent ski areas sometimes feel far safer in heeding the local weather prophets than they do in depending upon the metropolitan meteorological magicians.

MARCH

March, the season of the Spring equinox and the beginning of the agricultural year, was the first month of the Roman calendar for many years until New Year's day was moved to January 1 under Julius Caesar's reform. In the early Christian world after 400 A.D., the first of the year moved again—this time to March 25th, exactly nine months before Christmas or the Annunciation of the Virgin Mary. In the 16th century the new year again began with January, although in early American colonial days, March was still considered the first of the year.

In the early Roman days March was named for Mars, the god of war, since it was the month for military campaigns.

The snow geese have joined with the Canadas in their flight North. The osprey are back, and fox sparrows and mockingbirds are returning. Bluebirds and robins are frequently seen now. If they have stayed through the winter, other early arrivers are nuthatches, woodpeckers, finches, chickadees, crows, and jays. This month the puddleducks appear, and if warm enough, the woodcock will return. The phoebe arrives this month, ahead of other members of the flycatcher family.

FLOWERS:

You can begin to upgrade a bluegrass fescue lawn now; seed and fertilizer can be spread on top of the snow. When the forsythia blooms it is time to apply pre-emergence crabgrass killer.

Prepare the soil and sow seeds as soon as the soil can be worked for: poppies, larkspur, cornflowers, sweet peas, spinach, kale, mustard, and peas. Two weeks later sow seeds for: lettuce, radishes, turnips, Swiss chard, carrots, sweet alyssum, annual phlox, babies' breath, and cleome.

Flowering quince, trailing arbutus, forsythia, pussywillow, and Siberian Squill have bloomed, and the fragrant guelder reaches its height in March and early April.

SISTER LETTIE'S MAPLE PIE

INGREDIENTS:

2 tablespoons butter
1 cup maple sugar
1¼ cups hot milk
3 eggs

2 tablespoons cornstarch
⅛ cup cold milk
½ teaspoon salt
1 unbaked pastry shell
⅛ teaspoon nutmeg

DIRECTIONS:

Melt butter and blend in maple sugar; gradually add hot milk and stir until sugar is well dissolved. Beat eggs, wet cornstarch with cold milk and blend with hot mixture. Add salt. Turn into unbaked pie shell and sprinkle with nutmeg. Bake in 350-degree oven until custard is set, or until a silver knife inserted into it comes out clean.

MARCH 2

At the birdfeeder this morning were eleven chickadees and two squirrels. This is an unending battle between the squirrels and me, and they seem to take considerable delight in raiding my feeder of the sunflower seeds. Now when I rap on the window they just stand very still and look at me. It is only when I open it and shake my fist at them in mock anger that they scurry off into my forsthia bush, or go lickity-split across the crusted snow into the woods in back of my house.

MARCH 4

It was March 4, 1929 that I went to our notorious capitol to see Herbert Hoover inaugurated. The entire trip is full of poignant memories for me for at that time I was a very young lad and because my father and mother had moved from the country to the Big City, it seemed wise for them to put me in a small private boarding school which was located in the Hudson Highlands of New York State. This whole school experience was something brand new for me as I had never been away from home before.

Well, anyway, 2 special cars on the train took us from Poughkeepsie to the Grand Central Station in New York City, where we would be transported by bus across town to the Pennsylvania Station and then on to the Baltimore & Ohio to continue our journey.

If there was one emotion that I suffered from greatly in those tender years, it was homesickness. My mother and I had always been great pals and I was feeling rather dejected over the idea that I was passing through the city and would not be able to see her. Just imagine my surprise and delight as we were passing through Grand Central to find her waiting for me. I can still remember how we both cried a little and I can recall the scent of the cologne that she used. Of course it was a little embarrassing with all the fellows looking on, but at the moment I was willing to put up with that just for the joy of seeing her.

I don't remember too much about the inauguration except that we dropped bags of water out of the hotel room onto people walking on the sidewalks below, and that Mr. Hoover wore a very shiny silk top hat. It seemed a little ridiculous in the middle of the day.

MARCH 13

MIST

Low-anchored cloud,
Newfoundland air,
Fountain-head and source of rivers,
Dew-cloth, dream-drapery,
And napkin spread by fays;
Drifting meadow of the air,
Where blooms the daisied banks and violets,
And in whose fenny labyrinth
The bittern booms and heron wades;
Spirit of lakes and seas and rivers,
Bear only perfumes and the scent
Of healing herbs to just men's fields.

HENRY DAVID THOREAU

COLORS

Blue is true,
Yellow's jealous,
Green's forsaken,
Red's brazen,
White is love's breath.

MARCH 21

Regardless of what the calendar may say, I know that spring is here because today my L.L. Bean Catalog arrived! What a plethora of reminders that the outdoor season is beckoning from beyond your snow laden bush. I may never get into a canoe again, but Bean's canoe moccasin described in terse, descriptive prose will always intrigue me, and where else can I get a trapper's moccasin or a country walker or trap and skeet shoe?

But I see that along with the insulated hunting shoes, fly rods, dry flys, fly boxes, spinning reels, tackle bags and foot waders, there are new items that indicate that perhaps with Bean's the old will never change but nevertheless they, too, from their refuge in Freeport, Maine, recognize that there are changes. These include cowboy hats, warm-up suits, Australian bush hats, ladies' bandanna shirts, walking shorts, and a book on walking. Can you imagine the consternation of one who has dropped from the L.L. Bean mailing list? I'd rather be drummed out of the Union League Club.

MARCH 27

I happened to notice that March is the month to commemorate many diversified events. For example, on the 5th of March in 1770 the Boston Massacre took place. It is now rather interesting that the later research on this event has raised a question or two as to just who was at fault and what really did happen. On the 12th of March, Juliet Lowe founded the Girl Scouts, thereby giving us all a chance to partake of some of the most delicious cookies for miles around.

Julius Caesar failed to beware of the Ides of March and supplied W. Shakespeare with the material for one of his most powerful plays. I understand that the Vatican has decannonized St. Patrick but this is one of the most celebrated days of the year, particularly in New York City.

I personally am looking at the American Bicentennial celebration with a mildly jaundiced eye. Philadelphia has already given up its big plans; Boston has done the same, but according to reports we can look forward to a tremendous surge of people towards the northeast in 1975 and 1976. Among the other happenings in 1775 was Patrick Henry's famous "Liberty or Death Speech" which took place in the Virginia House of Burgesses on March 23rd.

Elizabeth Barrett Browning, Oliver Wendell Holmes, Paul Verlaine, and William Morris (the writer, not the agent) were all born in March. I wonder how many of these Morris, the agent, would have taken on in his day?

MARCH 29

On Saturday afternoon I had had the joyous experience of attending a country wedding. I say country wedding because it was rather informal as weddings go. Everyone wore neat clothing, and the bride did have on her grandmother's dress, but she had draped many garlands of flowers over her bodice. On the other hand the groom had a pair of neatly washed blue jeans and a tweed coat. He too, had garlands of flowers around his neck. I thought they had as reasonable a chance as anyone else to enjoy many years of nuptial bliss.

When it comes to marriage, Oscar Wilde is probably one of the most frequently quoted cynics on the subject. Here are a few of his choice bon mots:

"Men marry because they are tired; women because they are curious; both are disappointed."

"The amount of women in London who flirt with their own husbands is perfectly scandalous. It looks so bad. It's simply washing one's clean linen in public."

"The happiness of a married man depends on the people he has not married."

"A family is a terrible incumbrance, especially when one is not married."

"Twenty years of romance make a woman look like a ruin; but twenty years of marriage make her look like a public building."

"In married life affection comes when people thoroughly dislike each other."

"There is nothing in the world like the devotion of a married woman. It is a thing no married man knows anything about."

MARRIAGE
When a man has married a wife, he finds out whether
Her knees and elbows are only glued together.
WILLIAM BLAKE

Mirror, Mirror, tell me,
*   Am I pretty or plain?*
Or am I downright ugly
*   And ugly to remain?*
Shall I marry a gentleman?
*   Shall I marry a clown?*
Or shall I marry old Knives- and Scissors
*   Shouting through the town?*

Now you're married you must obey;
You must be true to all you say;
You must be kind; you must be good;
And keep your wife in kindling wood.

Needles and pins, needles and pins,
When a man marries his trouble begins.

P. BRVEGEL. INVENT

Locht op speelman ende latet wel dueren,
  Soo langh als de lul ghaet en den rommel vermach
Doet lyse wel dapper haer billen rueren,
  Want ten is vry met haer gheen gruyloft . alden dach

2.   *Wedding Dance* by Peter Bruegel, the Elder

Vents

Nu hebbelyck hannen danst soomen plach,
   Ick luyster na de pijp en ghy mist den voete:
aer ons bruyt neemt nu van dansen verdrach,
   Trouwens, tis oock best, want sy ghaet vol en soete.

TRIVIA

THE OPTIMIST
The optimist fell ten stories.
  At each window bar
He shouted to his friends:
  "All right so far."

UP IN THE NORTH
Up in the north, a long way off,
The donkey's got the whooping-cough.

EPITAPH ON A DENTIST
Stranger, approach this spot with gravity;
John Brown is filling his last cavity.

ON RICHARD DENT, LANDLORD
Here lies Richard Dent
In his cheapest tenement.

I asked my mother for fifty cents
To see the elephant jump the fence;
He jumped so high
He reached the sky,
And never came back till the Fourth of July.

I do not love thee, Doctor Fell,
  The reason why I cannot tell;
But this I know, I know full well:
  I do not love thee, Doctor Fell.

SIGNS, SEASONS, AND SENSE
Thirty days hath September,
April, June, and November.
All the rest have thirty-one,
Except Febuary alone,
Which has four and twenty-four
Till leap-year gives it one day more.

Monday's child is fair of face,
Tuesday's child is full of grace,
Wednesday's child is full of woe,
Thursday's child has far to go,
Friday's child is loving and giving,
Saturday's child works hard for a living,
And a child that's born on the Sabbath day
Is fair and wise and good and gay.

See a pin and pick it up,
All day you'll have good luck.
See a pin and let it lie,
You'll be sorry by and by.

Multiplication is vexation,
Division is as bad;
The Rule of Three it puzzles me,
And Fractions drive me mad.

TRIVIA

APRIL

April probably derived its name from the Latin verb aperire, meaning "to open." Its name is also associated with the Greek word "aphros," the root word of "Aphrodite," the Greek goddess of love to whom the month was sacred.

To poets and other literary figures throughout the ages, April has traditionally been a symbol for inconstancy and rain. Thus the month has inspired many a work of art, not to mention the old wives' tale—"Those born in the month of April are the most robust."

BIRDS:

The winter wren and northern water thrush arrive in early April. Two weeks later the hermit thrush and house wren return, along with tree, fox, and song sparrows, blue herons, and blue-winged teals. As the birds return to their summer residence, the males, who usually arrive ahead of the females, set territories before courtship and mating can begin.

If you wish to build a birdhouse or nesting box, know the proper dimensions of the house and the size of the entrance for the bird you want to attract. Place the house in the bird's natural habitat and allow for ventilation for those houses that are placed in the sun. Use a weathered wood to make the bird house less conspicuous (unless it is to be a purple martin apartment house). If well-seasoned wood is unavailable, a wood preservative stain produces the same effect. Use a thick wood for its insulating value.

FLOWERS:

April is the time to heavily seed the bare spots of your yard and the rest of the lawn lightly. Feed bluegrass fescue lawns now. Shrubs and trees are best transplanted early this month while they are still dormant. Prune crowded, crossed, or winter-damaged branches of shrubs before new growth begins.

After the last frost, plant seeds for: aster, morning glory, marigold, zinnia, balsam, dahlias (tubers), and gladiolas (corms). Beans, cucumber, basil, dill, pumpkin, squash, and corn can also be planted at this time.

Spicebush, andromeda, rhododendron, dogwood, magnolia, shadbush, evergreen boxwood, and clove currant are blossoming. Hyacinths, tulips, daffodils, Spring daphnes, and bluebells are in bloom in gardens. Bloodroot, marsh marigolds, and violets grow wild. And columbine, mandrake, wood anemone, viburnum, and jonquil dot woods or shaded garden areas with color.

FLOWER FROST GUIDE:

When daffodils, forsythia, and flowering quince bloom, there is still danger of frost.

When apple blossoms and dogwood blossoms are out, there is not much danger of a frost (not guaranteed).

When oak trees leaf, the danger of a frost is over, aside from an unusual freak cold snap.

APRIL 1

This is the day upon which we are reminded of what we are on the other three hundred and sixty-four.

MARK TWAIN

APRIL 2

I'm always lulled into a false sense of security each year with the arrival of the first day of April. Of course, we all know that Nature really doesn't pay any attention to the calendar, so the official arrival of Spring during the last week of March can be ignored. However, we are all quite willing to concede that winter is over especially if somewhere during the first days of April there is a sudden change in weather and we see crocuses and daffodils poking up.

And then it snows. We've had some of the most substantial snows of the winter during the second week of April. Among the things that cause it is the fact that people take their snow tires off during the first week in April, or they start raking their lawns. These two factors alone have been known to be the cause of 8-inch snowfalls on Palm Sunday.

Another cause of snow in April is the removal of the golf clubs from the attic and even desultory swings with a mashie niblick on the half frozen ground.

There is a lady of my acquaintance who personally caused a four day cold snap in April by wearing a straw bonnet to the post office with spring flowers on it.

You have got to be careful what you do during the first week of April.

APRIL 7

AMORETTI

Fresh Spring, the herald of loves mighty king,
In whose cote-armor richly are displayed
All sorts of flowers the which on earth do spring,
In goodly colors gloriously arrayd,
Goe to my love, where she is carelesse layd,
Yet in her winters bowre, not well awake;
Tell her the joyous time wil not be staid,
Unlesse she doe him by the forelock take:
Bid her therefore her selfe soone ready make,
To wayt on Love amongst his lovely crew,
Where every one that misseth then her make
Shall be by him amearst with penance dew.
Make hast therefore, sweet love, whilest it is prime;
For none can call againe the passed time.

EDMUND SPENSER

HOME-THOUGHTS FROM ABROAD

Oh, to be in England
Now that April's there,
And whoever wakes in England
Sees, some morning, unaware,
That the lowest boughs and the brushwood sheaf
Round the elm-tree bole are in tiny leaf,
While the chaffinch sings on the orchard bough
In England — now!
And after April, when May follows,
And the whitethroat builds, and all the swallows?
Hark, where my blossomed pear-tree in the hedge
Leans to the field and scatters on the clover
Blossoms and dewdrops — at the bent spray's edge—
That's the wise thrush; he sings each song twice over,
Lest you should think he never could recapture
The first fine careless rapture!
And though the fields look rough with hoary dew,
All will be gay when noontide wakes anew
The buttercups, the little children's dower
—Far brighter than this gaudy melon-flower!

ROBERT BROWNING

WEATHER

This is the weather the cuckoo likes,
    And so do I;
When showers benumble the chestnut spikes,
    And nestlings fly;
And the little brown nightingale bills his best,
And they sit outside the "Traveller's Rest,"
And maids come forth sprig-muslin drest,
And citizens dream of the South and West,
    And so do I.

This is the weather the shepard shuns,
    And so do I:
When beeches drip in browns and duns,
    And thresh, and ply;
And hill-hid tides throb, throe on throe,
And meadow rivulets overflow,
And drops of gate-bars hang in a row,
And rooks in families homeward go,
    And so do I.

THOMAS HARDY

APRIL 14

Yesterday morning I found myself on one of the interstate highways leading from our Berkshire Hills here in Massachusetts through the gently rolling farm and woodland of New York State. It was a gorgeous morning, a little chilly, but with the chilliness of early spring that portends beautiful weather later on in the day. For quite a bit of the trip I felt almost alone on this road, as there were no cars visible either in front or behind. It was like being alone.

Almost.

For on my left I noticed an automobile parked behind one of the hummocks and with some kind of electronic equipment on the ground next to it. Sure enough, in just about a tenth of a mile there was a sign announcing the fact that radar scrutiny was going on just ahead. I looked at my speedometer and it registered exactly 60 miles an hour. So it was with some complacency that I traversed the line of cars on either side of the road that were pulled over by the minions of the state constabulary and would be in due time confronted with their crime by the figures supplied on the computer.

This made me realize that there are literally hundreds of thousands of drivers who because of this more impersonal, efficient method of apprehending speeders, will never know the absolute terror and constriction of abdomen muscles that come when, at going 80, they look through the rear view mirror to see the blinking red light and hear the screech of the siren. It made instant believers out of even the most hardened agnostics.

APRIL 27

With the exception of the crucifixion of Jesus which may not have taken place in April at all, the most important of the many events that took place during this month was probably the birth of William Shakespeare in April, 1564. For example, Admiral Perry reached the North Pole in April, 1909, General Lee surrendered at Appamatox in 1865, the Civil War began at Fort Sumter in 1861. Abraham Lincoln was assasinated in April, 1865, and of course, Paul Revere made the famous ride in April, 1775.

A great many of these events did, in fact, change the course of history but over the long run Shakespeare's plays will have a far greater affect on the world in thousands of years to come than any of these previously mentioned.

A SEXTETTE OF
SONNETS

By
WILLIAM SHAKESPEARE

✠

XVIII

Shall I compare thee to a summer's day?
Thou art more lovely and more temperate.
Rough winds do shake the darling buds of May,
And summer's lease hath all too short a date.
Sometime too hot the eye of heaven shines,
And often is his gold complexion dimmed.
And every fair from fair sometimes declines,
By chance of nature's changing course untrimmed.
But thy eternal summer shall not fade,
Nor lose possession of that fair thou owest,
Nor shall death brag thou wander'st in his shade
When in eternal lines to time thou grow'st.
　　So long as men can breathe, or eyes can see,
　　So long lives this, and this gives life to thee.

XLIX

Against that time, if ever that time come,
When I shall see thee frown on my defects,
When as thy love hath cast his utmost sum,
Called to that audit by advised respects—
Against that time when thou shalt strangely pass,
and scarcely greet me with that sun, thine eye,

When love, converted from the thing it was,
Shall reasons find of settled gravity—
Against that time do I ensconce me here
Within the knowledge of mine own desert,
And this my hand against myself uprear,
To guard the lawful reasons on thy part.
  To leave poor me thou hast the strength of laws,
  Since why to love I can allege no cause.

LXXXVIII

When thou shalt be disposed to set me light,
And place my merit in the eye of scorn,
Upon thy side against myself I'll fight,
And prove thee virtuous, though thou art forsworn.
With mine own weakness being best acquainted,
Upon thy part I can set down a story
Of faults concealed, wherein I am attainted,
That thou in losing me shalt win much glory.
And I by this will be a gainer too,
For bending all my loving thoughts on thee,
The injuries that to myself I do,
Doing thee vantage, double-vantage me.
  Such is my love, to thee I so belong
  That for thy right myself will bear all wrong.

XCI

Some glory in their birth, some in their skill,
Some in their wealth, some in their body's force,
Some in their garments, though newfangled ill,
Some in their hawks and hounds, some in their
    horse.
And every humor hath his adjunct pleasure,
Wherein it finds a joy above the rest.
But these particulars are not my measure,
All these I better in one general best.
Thy love is better than high birth to me,

Richer than wealth, prouder than garments' cost,
Of more delight than hawks or horses be.
And having thee, of all men's pride I boast,
  Wretched in this alone, that thou mayst take
  All this away and me most wretched make.

XLVIII

How careful was I when I took my way,
Each trifle under truest bars to thrust,
That to my use it might unused stay
From hands of falsehood, in sure words of trust!
But thou, to whom my jewels trifles are,
Most worthy comfort, now my greatest grief,
Thou, best of dearest and mine only care,
Art left the prey of every vulgar thief.
Thee have I not locked up in any chest,
Save where thou art not, though I feel thou art,
Within the gentle closure of my breast,
From whence at pleasure thou mayst come and part.
  And even thence thou wilt be stol'n, I fear,
  For truth proves thievish for a prize so dear.

CVI

When in the chronicle of wasted time
I see descriptions of the fairest wights,
And beauty making beautiful old rhyme
In praise of ladies dead and lovely knights,
Then, in the blazon of sweet beauty's best,
Of hand, of foot, of lip, of eye, of brow,
I see their antique pen would have expressed
Even such a beauty as you master now.
So all their praises are but prophecies
Of this our time, all you prefiguring,
And, for they looked but with divining eyes,
They had not skill enough your worth to sing.
  For we, which now behold these present days,
  Have eyes to wonder, but lack tongues to praise.

MAY

The month of May was possibly named for the Greek goddess Maia, the mother of Hermes, or from Maia Majesta, a local Italian goddess of Spring to whom sacrifices were made to insure crop growth. Also

Romulus assigned the month of May to the elders or "majores" who gave counsel, and thus another possible derivation of the name "May."

It is a month associated with new vegetation and has been traditionally ushered in by May Day celebrations. Although at one point the Puritans uprooted all of the May-poles which brought all May Day festivities to a screeching halt, after the Restoration, May 1st was again a day of celebration.

BIRDS:

May is the month the warblers return in flocks. Bobolinks, catbirds, ovenbirds, scarlet tanagers, indigo buntings, whip-poorwills, and rose-breasted grosbeaks have arrived by now. The oriole has one of the most precise timing schedules and will return almost within the same hour of the same day in May every year. Waves of shorebirds may linger in the area on their way north to summer residence, and the last of the fly-catchers arrive. The birds are nesting at this time.

FLOWERS:

Apply mulches in the garden and flower beds to control weeds and retain moisture. Select plants of phlox, primrose and impatiens from the nursery. Set out plants of tomatoes, chrysanthemums, snap dragons, petunias, eggplant, and peppers now. Sow seeds for sunflowers and other late summer bloom.

The fruit trees reach their peak of blossoming this month. Viburnum, wisteria, iris, bleeding heart, peonies, clematis, and mock orange fill the gardens and trellises with color. And by the end of May the lilac has bloomed and the lilies-of-the-valley are out. In the forest, Jack-in-the-pulpit, pink lady slippers, mayflowers, Dutchman's breeches appear, and violets abound in the fields and woods.

SHAKER JELLIED VEAL

INGREDIENTS

4 veal shanks, split	1 blade of mace
2 quarts water	2 stalks celery, minced
1/8 teaspoon pepper	8 sprigs parsley, minced
1 teaspoon salt	1 carrot, cooked and minced
1 bay leaf	1 tablespoon green pepper, minced
1 teaspoon chervil, cut	

DIRECTIONS

Boil the split veal shanks with the seasoning slowly for 3 hours. Separate the meat into shreds. When the pot-liquor is cold, strain until clear and pour over meat in mold to which the minced vegetables and herbs have been added. Chill until jellied. This can be cut into slices and served on a bed of lettuce leaves as a salad or served as a cold meat.

MAY 1

Fo lo, the winter is past, the rain is over and gone;

The flowers appear on the earth; the time of the singing of birds is come, and the voice of the turtle is heard in our land;

The fig tree putteth forth her green figs, and the vines with the tender grape give a good smell. Arise, my love, my fair one, and come away.

SONG OF SOLOMON 2:11-13

FROM CORINNA'S GOING A-MAYING

Get up, get up for shame, the blooming morn
Upon her wings presents the god unshorn.
See how Aurora throws her fair
Fresh-quilted colors through the air:
Get up, sweet slug-abed, and see
The dew bespangling herb and tree.
Each flower has wept and bowed toward the east
Above an hour since! yet you not dressed;
Nay! not so much as out of bed?
When all the birds have matins said
And sung their thankful hymns, 'tis sin,
Nay, profanation, to keep in,
When as a thousand virgins on this day
Spring, sooner than the lark, to fetch in May.

ROBERT HERRICK

TODAY AND TOMORROW

Happy the man, and happy he alone,
*   He who can call today his own;*
He who, secure within, can say,
*   Tomorrow, do thy worst, for I have lived today!*

JOHN DRYDEN

MAY 5

Today was the kind of day that makes me think of my Uncle George. He was one of the world's great guys. I used to go and visit my Aunt Zelma and him at their home in a little town in upstate New York where my Uncle George was an employee of the railroad. I particularly remember the year I graduated from grammar school, I spent the summer with them. Aunt Zelma and I used to sit on the front porch of their home which was on a busy road and we would play 500 Rummy at any hour of the morning or afternoon. Then we played games trying to identify automobiles. She was a real pal.

About three-thirty each afternoon my aunt would say: "It's time for your Uncle George to be coming to the gate." We would stop everything and I would get on my bike and pedal

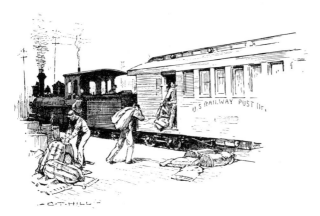

over to the railroad shop gate about a quarter of a mile away, where my Uncle George, who was a man with very white hair and a habitual sniff, would appear carrying his black lunch box, and we would go back to the house, I pushing my bicycle and he telling me about the various things that happened during the day. He was an expert on wrecks, and was very frequently called in the middle of the night to go on the wreck train to tell them how to get the cars back on the tracks.

Around five o'clock in the afternoon my aunt would announce that supper (it was always supper) was served and we ate in the summer kitchen which was really their back porch where a kerosene stove, which did not give out too much heat, was used to cook the frankfurters and baked beans or soup.

One of the great things about my uncle was that he owned an old 1926 Buick which he used to leave in the driveway, and it was understood that I could drive it up and down the driveway, but of course, not go into the street or through the end of the garage! I really learned to drive on that car that summer. There was a girl who lived up the road a little way and she used to come over and we both sat in the car and drove up and down the driveway all day. That's when I stopped playing 500 Rummy with my aunt!

SPRING SONG
From *PIPPA PASSES*

The year's at the spring
And the day's at the morn;
Morning's at seven;
The hillside's dew-pearled;
The lark's on the wing;
The snail's on the thorn;
God's in his heaven—
All's right with the world!

ROBERT BROWNING

UPON A DELAYING LADY

Come, come away,
Or let me go;
Must I here stay
Because y'are slow,
And will continue so?
Troth lady, no.

I scorn to be
A slave to the state:
And since I'm free
I will not wait,
Henceforth at such a rate,
For needy fate.

If you desire
My spark should glow,
The peeping fire
You must blow,
Or I shall quickly grow
To Frost or Snow.

From *CYMBELINE*

Hark, hark! the lark at heaven's gate sings,
    And Phoebus 'gins to arise,
His steeds to water at those springs
    On chaliced flowers that lies;
And winking Mary-buds begin
    To ope their golden eyes:
With every thing that pretty is,
    My lady sweet, arise;
        Arise, arise.

SHAKESPEARE

MAY 15

Once upon a time there was a very lovely lady who lived in a small city in upstate New York who owned a business upstairs across the street from three 5 & 10 cent stores. Every Saturday morning she used to watch an elderly lady attempt to drag a 4 year old kid past those stores. Such a caterwauling, wailing, fussing, tantrums and flailing has never been seen before or since. Almost every Saturday this same lovely lady that I mentioned earlier vowed: "If that kid was mine I'd beat him within an inch of his life."

While this continuing drama was going on every Saturday, the aforementioned lady was keeping company with a widower who had a very young son whom she had never met. The widower had been pressing his suit rather vigorously, but the lady in question was still undecided.

One day as she was walking through the residential section of town who does she come upon but this same harum-scarum kid from the 5 & 10 cent store riding on his tricycle. So she stopped and passed the time of day, and who do you think the kid turned out to be? Right. He was the son of the man whom she was giving serious consideration to marrying.

For reasons that I have never thoroughly ever understood, a short time later she agreed to marry the man and became an instant mother to a 4 year old terror on wheels. There are some things in the world that just simply can't be understood.

One of the first things she did was to take that kid downtown, past the 5 & 10 cent stores, and promise him that if he let out one squeak she would skin him alive. The kid never peeped.

And did that kid grow up to be the President of the United States? He did not. He grew up to be me.

MAY 28

A lot of interesting things happened in May. For example, the famous Scopes Trial took place in May 1925. Just one year later Admiral Richard Byrd flew over the North Pole. It hardly seems possible that that is such a short time ago. Israel became an independent state in May, 1948, and the Golden Gate Bridge was opened in May, 1937.

On May 19, 1910 Haley's Comet appeared and probably was the most spectacular event of the first ten years of the twentieth century.

However, May is famous for many other things including the Kentucky Derby and as being the month of the birthdays of Richard Wagner, John F. Kennedy, Walt Whitman, Honoré de Balzac, Ralph Waldo Emerson, and Robert Browning.

Tips on Bicycling

To fix a thrown chain, put the chain on the rear sprocket first. Press a few of the links down over the teeth at the top of the front sprocket and push the pedals forward, still holding the links in place. The chain should pop into place.

Replace a tire tube if it has a hole larger than the size of a pinprick. Otherwise patch it.

Most often slipping gears is caused by lubricating and adjusting them improperly.

When gears stick, check the cable; if it is frayed, it needs to be replaced. Also check the housing ends for grit and kinks.

To avoid changer problems in 10 speed bikes, do not lay the bike down on its right side, and do not back pedal when changing gears.

Before riding, check the air-pressure of the tires. Never ride on soft or flat tires to avoid damaging the rims.

After a ride, let a little pressure out of the tires to prevent an unexpected blowout.

A dry chain may slip or throw. Keep it oiled.

Always check the big axle nuts, wing nuts, and the quick release levers that hold the wheels to the frame. They should be tight.

When braking—apply both the rear and front handbrakes, increasing the pressure on the front brake until stopped.

On a long bike trip set a pace for yourself and stick to it. To keep muscles in tone avoid long stops for eating and resting. If you must stop, do so for a short time only.

Make sure your seat, frame, and stem extension are properly fitted to you to prevent back and wrist aches.

When riding at night wear a French arm-band light or use a head light and tail reflector.

When camping also, keep the load light and well-balanced.

On long trips take a spare tube and two tire-irons or a patch kit, a water bottle, a pump, a screw driver, and a crescent wrench.

JUNE

As Romulus had assigned May to the elders, he also assigned June to the youth or the "juniores" who fought in battles, from whence the month most probably derived its name.

While May was always considered the unlucky month for marriages in early Roman days because of the festivals of the unhappy dead and of the goddess of chastity, the Romans consequently believed June to be the most favorable. This belief has apparently survived as indicated by the numerous "White Sales" which occur just in time to fill the June brides' hope chests.

June was not only a month for weddings (and now White Sales) but it was also the month the cows could be milked three times instead of two. With this phenomenon alone to the Anglo-Saxons, June merited the name "Thricemilce."

BIRDS:

In June, insects are plentiful, and the swallows, in particular, help to control their population. June is the busiest month for the adult birds, since by now their young have hatched and need feeding. While most birds are caring for their young, the redwing and brown creeper are just beginning to nest. Because of this bird activity, June is the best month for birdwatching, and there is a wealth of summer birdlife in New England. Among the most commonly seen and heard are cardinals, hawks, orioles, wrens, sparrows, swallows, warblers, chimney swifts, robins, chickadees, and mocking birds.

FLOWERS:

In the garden the roses and lilies bloom in early June. Wild daisies and buttercups are rampant in the fields, and the wild strawberries are ready to be picked. In the woodlands, mountain laurel, clintonia, forget-me-nots and pinxter flowers are blooming, and the wild mint has begun to grow.

In gardens and lawn, maintenance dominates the program in June. Controlling weeds and insects and feeding plants is very important and can be done organically. For example, plant garlic around rose bushes to control insect pests and plant marigolds in your vegetable garden.

BURDOCK ROOTS:

Dig the roots of a first year Burdock (the first-year plant produces no flower stalk and can be easily recognized). Peel and slice thinly. Add a pinch of soda to the water, and boil the sliced roots for thirty minutes. Drain and boil for another thirty minutes. Season with butter and salt.

WILD STRAWBERRY SHORTCAKE

2 cups biscuit mix	1 quart wild strawberries
2 tablespoons sugar	½ pint whipped cream
¾ cups light cream	

Mix the biscuit mix, sugar and cream well. Turn the dough out onto a floured surface and knead until smooth. Divide the dough in half. Roll one half to fit a 9-inch pie plate. Brush the top with melted butter. Roll the second half to the same size and place on top. Bake in a pre-heated oven at 350-degrees for 20 minutes.

When cooled, lift off the top layer. Spoon ½ of the strawberries (which have been hulled and sugared) onto the first layer of the cake and top with ½ of the whipped cream. Replace the second layer on top and spoon the remaining strawberries and whipped cream on top of all.

JUNE 3

When I was a kid we moved several times in the small city in which I lived, and this meant that I was forever going back to visit my chums in the old neighborhood. One year, after we had moved to the other side of town, and I was still the New Kid, and got tired of batting last or being the first one to be "it" for the hide and seek games, I suggested to my mother that I would like to go back and visit Charles Cramer. She countered with the idea that Charles was really never a very good friend of mine, and why didn't I go outside and play with the other kids and get to know them better.

Well this only added fuel to the fire and I spent five minutes telling her what a great playmate Charles was, and how I was sure that we would have a wonderful time back in the old neighborhood.

She acquiesced, called Mrs. Cramer, whom none of us knew very well, but the arrangement was made and I was dropped off at his home the next morning complete with my BB gun and a thousand BB's, as it was planned that Charles and I would go out into the fields and try to hit tin cans most of the day.

This all worked out pretty well and in fact Charles and I found a great many things in common which heretofore had remained hidden. Then Charles' mother came home (I never knew anything about Charles' father) and we all had supper and sat around on the front porch eating ice cream until the inevitable moment of bedtime came.

It was here that I got the Big Shock. In the first place, I was not to be put into a bedroom where Charles and I would sit up all night talking. No way. Charles slept in the same bed with his mother because they had a small house. However, when she suggested that all three of us get into what seemed to be a fairly large-sized bed, I certainly offered no objections.

The arrangement was very simple—Charles would sleep in the middle, I would sleep on the outside and she would sleep on the other side. However, there was more to it.

Charles, it appeared, had an Errant Kidney and there was a rubber sheet under the bottom sheet of our bed. Well, of course, I was always a sort of swashbuckler in those days, and so the three of us climbed into bed, his mother turned off the light and, wearied by the effects of climbing over hill and dale with BB guns, I soon fell asleep.

I was awakened almost immediately by the strident voice of Charles' mother calling: "Charles, get up and go to the bathroom." Whereupon he climbed over me and made his way to the convenience.

He soon returned, climbed back over me, and a somewhat disturbed calm settled. I felt as if I was taking this in my stride and fell asleep again, but it must have been an hour later when again I heard the magic words: "Charles, get up and go to the bathroom." We repeated the performance.

By this time disenchantment was setting in but I was almost too tired to care.

The next thing I knew the light in the bedroom was on, Charles and his mother were both sitting up in bed and Charles was crying. The "Great Inevitable" had happened. So all of us got out of bed, Charles went to the bathroom, which of course seemed rather unnecessary at this point, while his mother changed the sheets.

I never went back to sleep again, as I was certainly not going to be caught off base twice the same night. Never had the first faint streaks of dawn seemed so welcome. Although I was scheduled to remain at Charles' house for the entire day and possibly another night, I fibbed to his mother and told her I had a type of malaise, and my mother came and got me right after breakfast. I slept all day.

Now, when the moon is a ghostly galleon tossed upon cloudy seas, I can still hear those strident tones: "Charles, get up and go to the bathroom." My reaction is instant vex.

SUMER IS ICUMEN IN

Sumer is icumen in,
　　Lhude sing cuccu;
Groweth sed and bloweth med
　　And springeth the wude nu.
　　　Sing cuccu!

Ewe bleteth after lomb,
　　Lhouth after calve cu;
Bulluc sterteth, bucke verteth,
　　Murie sing cuccu!

Cuccu, cuccu, wel
　　Singes thu, cuccu:
　　Na swike thu naver nu;
Sing cuccu, nu,
　　Sing cuccu, sing cuccu, nu.
　　　　　　　ANONYMOUS

ON THE GRASSHOPPER AND THE CRICKET

Green little vaulter in the sunny grass,
Catching your heart up at the feel of June,
Sole voice that's heard amidst the lazy noon,
When even the bees lag at the summoning brass;
And you, warm little housekeeper, who class
With those who think the candles come too soon,
Loving the fire, and with your tricksome tune,
Nick the glad, silent moments as they pass;
O sweet and tiny cousins, that belong
One to the fields, the other to the hearth,
Both have your sunshine; both, though small, are strong
At your clear hearts; and both seem given to earth
To sing in thoughtful ears this natural song,
In doors and out, summer and winter—mirth.
　　　　　　　LEIGH HUNT

A generation of man is like a generation of leaves: the wind scatters some leaves upon the ground, while others the burgeoning wood brings forth—and the season of spring comes on. So of men one generation springs forth and another ceases.

From the *ILLIAD VI*
HOMER

Now learn a parable of the fig tree; when his branch is yet tender, and putteth forth leaves, ye know that summer is nigh:

St. Matthew 24:32

WHERE THE BEE SUCKS
Where the bee sucks, there suck I;
In a cowslip's bell I lie;
There I couch when owls do cry;
On the bat's back I do fly
After summer merrily:
Merrily, merrily, shall I live now
Under the blossom than hangs on the bough.

William Shakespeare

TO LUCASTA, ON GOING TO THE WARS
Tell me not, sweet, I am unkind,
*   That from the nunnery*
Of thy chaste breast and quiet mind
*   To war and arms I fly.*
True, a new mistress now I chase,
*   The first foe in the field;*
And with a stronge faith embrace
*   A sword, a horse, a shield.*
Yet this inconstancy is such
*   As thou too shalt adore;*
I could not love thee, dear,
*   so much,*
*   Loved I not honor more.*

Richard Lovelace

JUNE 29

In looking back over the month of June, I find that it has many intriguing commemorative dates. In 1862 General Lee was made commander of the Confederate Army of Northern Virginia, in 1872 the free delivery of mail in the United States was instituted. In 1775, the Battle of Bunker Hill took place, in 1885 the Statue of Liberty was received as a gift from France.

Custer's forces were massacred at Little Big Horn in June, 1876. Napoleon was defeated at Waterloo in 1815, the last shot of the Civil War was fired in 1865, and the ill-fated Treaty of Versailles was signed in 1919.

ETIQUETTE NEVERS

Etiquette—almost seems like an outmoded word now. Our Victorian forebearers thought that etiquette was a substitute for good manners and here are a list of some of the sometimes practical and sometimes ludicrous don'ts that were concocted a hundred years ago.

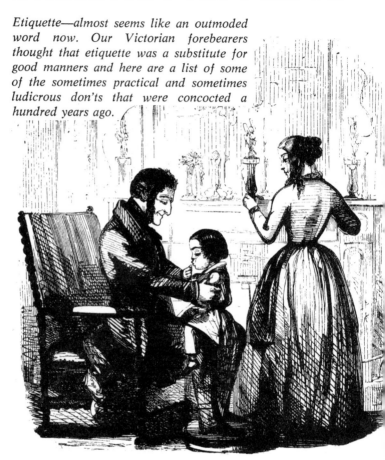

Never give all your pleasant words and smiles to strangers. The kindest words and the sweetest smiles should be reserved for home. Home should be your heaven.

> *"We have careful thought for the stranger*
> *And smiles for the sometimes guest;*
> *But oft for our own the bitter tone,*
> *Though we love our own the best.*
> *Ah! lips with the curl impatient—*
> *Ah! brow with the shade of scorn,*
> *'Twere a cruel fate were the night too late*
> *To undo the work of the morn."*

Never speak much of your own performances.

Never pick the teeth or clean the nails in company.

Never present a gift saying that it is of no use to yourself.

Never associate with bad company. Have good company or none.

Never arrest the attention of an acquaintance by a touch. Speak to him.

Never, when traveling abroad, be over-boastful in praise of your own country.

Never attempt to draw the attention of company constantly upon yourself.

Never enter a room noisily; never fail to close the door after you, and never slam it.

Never will a gentleman allude to conquests which he may have made with ladies.

Never send your guest, who is accustomed to a warm room, off into a cold, damp, spare bed to sleep.

Never enter a room filled with people without a slight bow to the general company when first entering.

Never accept favors and hospitalities without rendering an exchange of civilities when opportunity offers.

Never compel a woman with an infant in arms to stand while you retain your seat.

Never examine the cards in the card basket. While they may be exposed in the drawing-room, you are not expected to turn them over unless invited to do so.

Never should the lady accept expensive gifts at the hands of a gentleman not related or engaged to her. Gifts of flowers, books, music or confectionery may be accepted.

Never attempt to convey the impression that you are a genius by imitating the faults of distinguished men. Because certain great men were poor penmen, wore long hair, or had other peculiarities, it does not follow that you will be great by imitating their eccentricities.

JULY

July was originally called Quintilis because it was the fifth month of the Roman calendar. After trying numerous times (and failing) to have Julius Caesar named emperor, Mark Anthony finally succeeded in naming Caesar's birth month, July, in honor of him, two years after his assassination.

FLOWERS:

Day-lilies line the road and river banks, and black-eyed Susans and Queen Anne's lace grow wild in the fields. Bright red Cardinal flowers have bloomed in the woods, also the snake-root and white swamp azaleas.

It is a good time to start indoor herb gardens which will provide you with a fresh dill, parsley, or basil well into winter.

BIRDS:

With the young out of the nest, many birds are beginning second families in July. Although the cedar waxwings and gold-finches may just be starting their first families this late in the season.

TIPS FOR DRYING FLOWERS AND HERBS

It is very important to know when to cut the flowers for drying—cut them on a bright sunny day just before the flower reaches full maturity, though not after the color has begun to fade. Cutting time will be different for the various flowers. The plant will dry faster if you strip the stem of unnecessary parts.

Before hanging wild flowers to dry, recut their stems and strip them. Then place them in water for several hours to revive them. Hang a group of 4 or 5 stems upside down in any warm dry spot which has a good circulation of air. Do not expose them to direct sunlight.

Some popular wild flowers to dry are: black-eyed Susan, butterfly weed, bergamot, field daisy, Pearly Everlasting, golden rod, Queen Anne's lace, tansy, and thistles.

To dry herbs: cut them on a clear day when the sun is not too hot. There should be no dew on the herbs when cutting them. For herbs producing useful leaves (mint) cut before the flower opens. For herbs producing useful seeds (dill) cut before the seeds begin to drop. To insure growth the next season, do not cut more than a third of a perennial herb at a time. Hang them in a dry, shaded spot for 5 to 6 days or until the stem snaps easily. The flavor will be lost if they are left hanging too long, or if they are hung in sunlight or complete absence of light.

In a dried flower arrangement, stability is essential. Start an arrangement by attaching the taller pieces to a dowel pin (about 1/4" diameter). If this is firmly anchored, the remaining pieces can be inserted. For slender stems, reinforce with toothpicks, pipe cleaners, or florist sticks covered with florist tape. Use raffia or elastic bands to secure groups of small, thin stems. These groups can be inserted rather than each individual stem.

Ah, July and family picnics. Recently I was poring through an old photograph album maintained by my mother for many years, and one of its most poignant pages contained a permanent record of the day we all went to Columbia Crossroads, Pennsylvania in a 1923 Willis-Overland touring car to partake of the family picnic at one of my mother's sister's husband's families. You really didn't have to be a member of the family directly in line to be invited to those feasts. In fact, if you were good friends with the people next door they might invite you to their family picnic.

All the ladies in those days wore the traditional family picnic dress which was white linen. The pictures I have show my aunts and their friends, all a little overweight and somewhat busty, with their hair done in a knot on the back of their neck, standing around with great bowls of potato salad, pickled beets, mashed turnips and scalloped potatoes.

Anyway, on this particular day my father felt that because we were going to go down into the country, and the roads, while they were not concrete or blacktop, would not be as numerously traveled, it would be all right for my mother to drive. For a lady to drive in those days was almost like a lady smoking—you did it very privately.

As soon as we turned off the main road my father said, "Okay, you drive." My mother, game to the end, looked somewhat apprehensively at the one and one-half lanes of the dirt road, but nonetheless was willing to take a crack at it.

All progressed very well. In fact, she was having the time if her life pointing out the scenery with a toss of her head, and referring to some new barn or silo along the way. She had a comment about someone's orchard or flower garden, momentarily daring to remove her hand from its vise-like grip on the wheel. However, I knew that we were coming to the Styx, and there would be no Charon there to direct our crossing.

It looked innocent enough, this meandering stream. But the Bridge was in the offing. Many times we had driven across it with my father's firm hand on the wheel; the rumble of the wooden planks had clattered under our wheels creating a reasonable doubt as to whether or not they would hold up until we reached the opposite shore. There was no railing on this sylvan span, and the bridge itself was only about eight inches from the water. In late August when the stream was low you could drive into the brook and wash the car, which is a story for another time.

Well anyway, as we chugged up and down the low hills, through the forests and past the farmhouses, I knew I would not breathe easier until we had crossed this Rubicon. It came into sight and I remember my father admonishing my mother to remain calm and keep both hands on the wheel and just treat it like the regular roadway. He was the supreme optimist. Our front wheel hit the first plank and it sent forth that ominous rumble. Something gripped my mother akin to terror. She swerved to the left. My father pulled on the emergency brake and the front end of "Nellie" hung over the edge of the bridge with the left tire dabbling gently in the clear brook below.

For an instant or two we were all totally speechless, and I distinctly remember the lowing of a cow in the nearby field. For a moment we hung on the edge of the yawning abyss. Then my mother burst into tears and my father started laughing. For me, it was the most thrilling thing that had happened since I became sick on the roller coaster at Owasco Lake in Auburn, New York.

Well, we were just a short distance from the farm where we were having the family picnic, so my father walked over and all the men came back and some of them waded in the water up to their knees and pushed the car back on the bridge, while others weighted the back end of the car. In no time at all it was driven safely to our destination where all the kids thought I was something of a hero.

I don't think my mother ever drove again.

JULY 10

THE BEE

How doth the little busy bee
*   Improve each shining hour,*
And gather honey all the day
*   From every opening flower!*
How skillfully she builds her cell!
*   How neat she spreads the wax!*
And labors hard to store it well
*   With the sweet food she makes.*
In works of labor or of skill
*   I would be busy too;*
For Satan finds mischief still
*   For idle hands to do.*
In books, or work, or healthful play
*   Let my first years be past;*
That I may give for every day
*   Some good account at last.*

                                    ISAAC WATTS

God made bees,
*   And bees make honey.*
The miller's man does all the work—
*   But the miller makes the money.*

JULY 15

If we removed July from the calendar we would be missing out on some most interesting events of the past. For example, on the 1st of July in 1863 the Battle of Gettysburg started. John Paul Jones was born in 1747, and Washington, D.C. was chosen as the capitol of the United States in 1792. Bastille Day is celebrated by the French on July 14th and on July 20, 1969 the first U.S. astronauts walked on the moon.

Nathaniel Hawthorne Henry David Thoreau and Gerard Manley Hopkins were all born in July.

JULY 25

THE CITY MOUSE AND THE GARDEN MOUSE

The city mouse lives in a house;
The garden mouse lives in a bower,
He's friendly with the frogs and toads,
And sees the pretty plants in flower.
The city mouse eats bread and cheese;
The garden mouse eats what he can;
We will not grudge him seeds and stalks,
Poor little, timid, furry man.

CHRISTINA GEORGINA ROSSETTI

JULY 29

One, two
Buckle my shoe;
Three, four,
Shut the door;
Five, six,
Pick up sticks;
Seven, eight,
Lay them straight;
Nine, Ten,
A big fat hen;
Eleven, twelve,
Who will delve?
Thirteen, fourteen,
Maids a-courting;
Fifteen, sixteen,
Maids a-kissing;
Seventeen, eighteen,
Maids a-waiting;
Nineteen, twenty,
My stomach's empty.

What The Flowers Mean

ARCADIA, ROSE, *Friendship.*

ALMONDS, *Giddiness, heedlessness.*

AMETHYST, *Admiration.*

APPLE BLOSSOM, *Unchanging Friendship.*

BITTERSWEET NIGHTSHADE, *Truth.*

BLUE BELL, *Constancy.*

BUTTERCUP, *Riches; Memories of Childhood.*

CAMELLIA, *Gratitude; Perfect Loveliness.*

CARNATION, *Pure and deep love.*

CHICORY, *Frugality; Economy.*

CHRYSANTHEMUM, *A heart left to desolation.*

COREOPSIS, *Always cheerful.*

CROCUS, *Cheerfulness.*

FORGET-ME-NOT, *Do not forget.*

FOXGLOVE, *Insincerity; Occupation.*

FUCHSIA, *Taste; Frugality.*

GERANIUM, IVY, *I engage you for the next dance.*

GRAPE VINE, *Intemperance.*

HELIOTROPE, *I adore you; Devotion.*

HIBISCUS, *Delicate beauty.*

HYDRANGEA, *Vain-glory; Heartlessness.*

ICE PLANT, *Your looks freeze me.*

IVY, *Friendship; marriage.*

LAUREL, AMERICAN, *Words, though sweet, may deceive.*

LANTANA, *Rigor.*

LILAC, WHITE, *Youth.*

LILY, WHITE, *Majesty; Purity.*

LUPINE, *Dejection.*

MARSHMALLOW, *Beneficence.*

MINT, *Virtue.*

NIGHTSHADE, *Dark thoughts; Sorcery.*

PEONY, *Ostentation; Anger.*

PHLOX, *Our hearts are united.*

ROSE, RED, *I love you.*

ROSE, WHITE, *Silence.*

SORREL, *Parental Affection.*

STAR OF BETHLEHEM, *Reconciliation*

SUNFLOWER, *False riches.*

TULIP, RED, *Declaration of love.*

VERBENA, *Sensitivity.*

VIOLET, BLUE, *Faithfulness.*

YARROW, *Cure for the heartache.*

YEW, *Sadness.*

ZINNIA, *I mourn your absence.*

august

Since July was named for Julius, Augustus Caesar decided he too should have a month named in honor of him. Although September was his birth month, he decided upon August because it followed July, Julius' month, and most importantly because it was the month he was admitted to the consulate.

Although the name "August" is derived from the word augere, meaning to make greater and carries connotations of majesty and grandeur, many today can only associate August with the beginning of one and the end of another World War.

BIRDS:

August is a quiet month for birds and a slow time for bird-watching. Most of the birds have gone into seclusion during their post-nuptial molting, rarely singing or displaying themselves anymore. Territorial and marital bonds have given way to pre-migrational flocking, and great hordes of otherwise non-gregarious birds feed together, gaining strength for the coming winter.

Northern warblers arrive in New England and linger on their way south. A few of the bobolinks, swallows and flycatchers, the yellow warblers, blue-winged teals, and the shorebirds may already be heading south.

FLOWERS:

Mow a blue-grass fescue lawn with the blade one notch higher so the grasses can withstand a drought. Flood the basins of newly planted trees and shrubs and renew the mulch.

Thistles, milkweed, Joe-pye-weed, devil's paintbrushes, wild asters and golden rod fill fields and swamps with color. The annuals you planted for late-summer bloom are ready for cutting and lovely indoor arangements.

August 1 is Lammis Day and marks the end of the farming season. Make preparations for canning, freezing, and storing the harvest from your vegetable garden.

MILK WEED PODS:

Collect the hard, young pods. Cover them with boiling water and place over high heat. Boil for one minute, drain, and repeat this process 3 or 4 more times. The last time, boil for 12 minutes. Drain and season the pods.

SUNFLOWER SEEDS:

Take a quantity of sunflower seeds and break them up with a hammer, food chopper, or rolling pin. Fill a large container with water and scatter the broken seeds in it. Stir vigorously. The shells will remain floating and the kernels will fall to the bottom. Skim off the shells and drain the water from the kernels. The kernels then can be dried and roasted and used in a recipe which calls for nuts, or they can be ground into meal.

DRYING GOURDS:

Pick them after the first frost, when they are mature but not overripe. Wash them in soapy water, then in a common household disinfectant. Put a hole the size of a hatpin-prick in each end and hang by the stem in a cool place until you can hear the seeds when you shake the gourd.

AUGUST 7

Today was another Uncle George day. My Uncle George Berry who married my mother's sister, Zelma, was born and grew up in Gilette, Pennsylvania, which if I recall correctly, was named for the inventor of the safety razor. Anyway, there were a lot of Berry's in Gilette, and as far as I know, there still are. It was a great treat for me to be driven down there to meet these sort of unofficial cousins who lived on farms and one of whom owned a country store.

In those days farmers had a hard time getting along, especially between cash crops, so that my relatively city-bought outgrown clothes were always passed on to those two country cousins, and the twice a year trip down there always meant taking some things down for them and also bringing back baskets of apples, squash, turnips, carrots, and things like that.

I remember one day my uncle and I went for a long walk in the woods. This was the place that he grew up in as a boy, so he knew every tree and the story behind every abandoned home or cellar hole. He was a very gentle man who never for a moment would have thought of hunting the creatures in his woods. We would walk along for quite a ways, the pastoral silence broken only by his involuntary sniffing, and he would point to a large oak or beech tree and say: "Let's go over and look at that." There on the bark would be some faded carved initials and he would have a story or two to tell me about the owners. Never has a storyteller had such a rapt audience as he did on that golden October day.

My aunt had packed a lunch for us and it was my supreme delight to carry it in his battered black dinner pail which he used on weekdays working on the railroad.

We sat on a log and watched the leaves sifting down through the bars of sunlight and I can remember expressing my fears that at twelve I was worried about what I was going to do with my life. He put his hand on my head and said: "Boy, whatever you do I know it will turn out just fine."

Uncle George, I hope I've measured up.

AUGUST 24

Today is the birthday of Robert Herrick. Although the 17th century in England was the "Puritan century" and there were somewhat austere poets like Sidney and Spenser and Milton, there was an underground tendency away from the doctrines of predestination and devices of the devil. One of the rebel poets who had been associated with the Cavaliers was Robert Herrick.

I can just imagine some of the young swains of that time, fearful lest Cromwell's constabulary apprehend them, reading Herrick and Lovelace by the light of a hooded candle.

UPON JULIA'S CLOTHES
When as in silks my Julia goes,
Then, then, methinks, how sweetly flows
That liquidefaction of her clothes.
Next, when I cast mine eyes and see
That brave Vibration each way free;
O how that glittering taketh me!
ROBERT HERRICK

TO ANTHEA,
WHO MAY COMMAND HIM ANYTHING
Bid me to live, and I will live
   Thy Protestant to be,
Or bid me love, and I will give
   A loving heart to thee.
A heart as soft, a heart as kind,
   A heart as sound and free
As in the whole world thou canst find,
   That heart I'll give to thee.
Bid that heart stay, and it will stay
   To honour thy Decree:
Or bid it languish quite away,
   And't shall do for thee.
Bid me to weep, and I will weep
   While I have eyes to see:
And, having none, yet I will keep
   A heart to weep for thee.
Bid me dispair, and I'll despair
   Under that Cypress tree:
Or bid me die, and I will dare
   E'en Death to die for thee.
Thou art my life, my love, my heart,
   The very eyes of me:
And hast command of every part
   To live and die for thee.
ROBERT HERRICK

I had occasion this past week to pass once again through the city of Stroudsburg, Pa. and I reasoned that it was just about this time of year, some time ago, that I passed through Stroudsburg on still another infinitely more auspicious occasion.

I was about 14 years old. We had moved to the city, and my father and I had been "batching it" since my mother was visiting her sisters upstate. He and I decided one Friday night that it would be a real treat to visit my mother, and so about 10 p.m. we got in our automobile, the 1926 Buick which my Uncle George had left me in his will (to remain in the trust of my father until I was of sufficient age to own and drive it) and go across New Jersey through the Delaware Water Gap up through Pennsylvania and on to our old hometown.

As I recall, my father was "between jobs" and I don't believe that he had more than $12.58 in his pocket. However, gasoline was inexpensive and our hearts were high. I have always thought it great fun to leave for someplace in the middle of the night. We zoomed across New Jersey and soon approached signs indicating that we were not far from the Delaware Water Gap and Stroudsburg.

Then it happened. My father said, "I think our tire is going flat." We stopped the car, and sure enough it was. It wasn't a very good tire anyway. We changed it—I don't know how many of you gentle readers have ever changed a tire on a pre-1930 automobile, but it is a backbreaking, knuckle-rasping job that can only be done if you know the right genteel swear words. My father knew them all. About an hour later we were on our way again approaching Stroudsburg and the Delaware Water Gap.

Then it happened again. The spare, which was in worse condition than the tire we took off, had also blown. There was no other spare. There we were, at about 4 a.m. on a beautiful summer morning with very little cash and no spare tire.

I still remember how much fun it was to walk into town on the metal of the macadam, our steps echoing. There was a sweet smell of honeysuckle and the morning birds began their breakfast symphony. We walked over the bridge and into the deserted business block and started to search for some kind of a service station that might be able to accommodate us, but there were no lights and certainly no all-night gasoline emporiums.

I recall that we walked down one side of the street, and in the distance in the rapidly increasing morning light there was a sign that said "tire store." Sure enough. There it was. It was now 6 a.m. and my father read the note on the door which said that in case of an emergency one should call such-and-such a number, but he was loath to rouse the proprietor from his early morning sleep, and besides, it said that the store would be open at 7:30.

We sat on a bench in a little park facing the store and I don't remember now what we talked about, but I do remember that I had never felt as close to my father.

We began to guess which one of the people walking the street would be our man. After several bad guesses, he finally appeared and opened the store. We crossed over and went inside. It had the rubbery odor of tires and inner tubes. Keenly aware that our limited financial means might indicate that my father might have to do a bit of bargaining, I drifted discreetly to the far end of the store where there was a collection of shiny bicycles on sale. When the tone of their conversation indicated that some kind of an agreement had been reached, I wandered self-consciously back and my father sensing my mood, put his hand on my shoulder and said, "It's okay."

The tire store proprietor was kind enough to load the tire (we could only afford one) into his truck and he drove us the six or seven miles out of town to where our 1926 Buick was still serenely waiting.

My father and I did successfully negotiate the remainder of the trip with no further incidents, and, in fact, that particular tire remained on the car until another incident about five years later which can be recorded at some other time.

The memory of that wonderful night is still with me. It may just be one of the 13 most terrific nights of my life.

August 28

Two interestingly diverse men were born in August. One was Orville Wright, born in 1871, who changed the course of history along with his brother, Wilbur, with their developments of the flights of heavier-than-air-machines. The other was Davy Crockett, who was born in 1876 and provided enough material to change the course of television for at least ten years.

The American author, Herman Melville, was born in August, 1819 and Oliver Wendell Holmes, who is listed as an author and a physician, was born in 1829. Thomas de Quincy was born in August, 1785, and Alfred Tennyson in 1809.

Other notable August happenings include Columbus sailing for the New World in 1492. The first talking moving pictures were shown in August, 1926 and proved to be a boon to the popcorn manufacturers. Lincoln began debating Douglas in 1858, and the Civil War ended in August, 1865.

3. *Summer* by Peter Bruegel, the Elder

WEATHER

If bees stay at home,
Rain will soon come.
If they fly away,
Fine will be the day.

When the wind is in the East,
'Tis neither good for man nor beast;
When the wind is in the North,
The skillful fisher goes forth;
When the wind is in the South,
It blows the bait in the fishes' mouth;
When the wind is in the West,
Then 'tis at the very best.

When clouds appear like rocks and towers,
The earth's refreshed by frequent showers.
If woolly fleeces spread the heavenly way,
No rain, be sure, disturbs the summer's day.

Small showers last long, but sudden storms are short.
SHAKESPEARE
Richard II, II:i

Evening red and morning gray
Are the signs of a bonny day.
Evening gray and morning red
Bring down rain on the farmer's head.

When the days begin to lengthen,
Then the cold begins to strengthen.

Rainbow at night
Is the sailor's delight;
Rainbow at morning,
Sailor, take warning!

A sunshiny shower
Won't last an hour

Rain before seven,
Clear before eleven.

September

September was the seventh month of the Roman calendar, and thus its name is derived from the Latin word septem, meaning seven.

It is the harvest month and is traditionally the month of agricultural fairs where farmers show off their livestock and produce, and their wives display their needlework and canned goods.

The swallows, chimney swifts, and hummingbirds are the first to go south after the frost. Flycatchers, whippoorwills, cuckoos, orioles, bobolinks, blackbirds, vireos and osprey follow.

September is the month of the warbler migration south. Slate-colored juncos, however, are just arriving from the North.

FLOWERS:

It is an ideal time to start new lawns or upgrade old ones. You should plant peonies, oriental poppies, and bleeding hearts now since they are dormant during this season. Bulbs for early spring bloom—grape hyacinth, snowdrops, and winter aconite—can also be planted now.

The morning glories are in bloom, also the dahlias, autumn clematis, and chrysanthemums.

SHAKER CIDER PIE

½ cup boiled-down cider
1 tablespoon butter
1 cup maple sugar
¼ cup water
  dash of salt

2 egg yolks, beaten
2 egg whites, beaten
1 unbaked pie shell
  dash of nutmeg

Boil down cider until it is a rich, dark syrup. Take ½ cup of this and put in saucepan; add butter, sugar, water and a dash of salt, and simmer several minutes. Cool slightly and add beaten egg yolks; now fold in stiffly beaten egg whites. Pour into unbaked shell. Dust with nutmeg and bake until shell is brown and custard well set.

SHAKER CIDER SAUCE

1 tablespoon butter
¾ tablespoon flour

1½ cups cider, boiled down
2 tablespoons sugar

Blend butter and flour over low heat; add cider gradually, and stir smooth. Add sugar and boil 5 minutes. Serve hot.

SEPTEMBER 4

GYPSIES IN THE WOOD
My mother said that I never should
Play with the gypsies in the wood,
The wood was dark; the grass was green;
In came Sally with a tambourine,
I went to sea—no ship to get across;
I paid ten shillings for a blind white horse;
I up on his back and was off in a crack,
Sally, tell my mother I shall never come back.

ANONYMOUS

SEPTEMBER 6

HE WHO KNOWS
He who knows not,
and knows not that he knows not, is a fool. Shun him.
He who knows not,
and knows that he knows not, is a child. Teach him.
He who knows,
and knows not that he knows, is asleep. Wake him.
He who knows,
and knows that he knows, is wise. Follow him.

from THE PERSIAN

SEPTEMBER 9

Last night I was going through a box of old photographs, dance programs and love letters, when I ran across a priceless piece of memorabilia. Priceless only to me. It was a card that was issued to all freshman at my college which was used to indicate which fraternities would invite me to have either dinner or luncheon with them during fraternity Rushing Week.
time, because many colleges have phased out fraternities. However, for me the memory of that particular morning is still a treasured one.

I was in a freshman dormitory, and the night before the neophytes all gathered around talking about the fact that it was Rush Week, and would we join a fraternity if asked, and who would ask us. Some of us vowed to stick together no matter what happened, others were quite superior to the whole arrangement. I don't believe I slept two straight minutes for the entire night.

Sure enough, at 7 a.m. there came a pounding at my door and my roommate and I nearly knocked heads in our zest to open it first. There standing in front of us, resplendent with a houndstooth checked polo coat was one of the BMOC's. He represented one of the most prestigious fraternities on the campus. My heart leapt with joy and anticipation, and I tried to look as cool as possible in my pajamas.

He stood there looking at the two us for at least five full seconds, then brought out a notebook and consulted it and said, "Oh, I'm sorry, I think I have the wrong room."

That just may have been the most devastating dagger ever plunged into my ego.

SEPTEMBER 18
Today is the birthday of Dr. Samuel Johnson, who was born the son of a bookseller in Litchfield, England. It is reported that he read books instead of selling them, thereby doing his father's business no good whatsoever.

No man ever had a more undistinguished educational career, most of which had been provided by friends of his father. He married at the age of 26 a woman twenty years his senior, who possessed one thousand pounds of sterling.

I have always been intrigued by accounts of his life and the monumental task involved in compiling his Dictionary of the English Language. It took seven arduous years. Apparently he spent most of them at odds with his publisher because one of the best known stories relates that his publisher said, when he received the last sheet: "Thank God. I am done with him." Johnson's retort was: "I am glad he thanks God for anything."

He was the Alexander Wolcott of his day, and gathered with his peers at the various Queen Anne coffee houses, just as a later group of journalists and wits gathered at the Algonquin Roundtable in the early 1920's in New York.

It's doubtful that any of us would be as informed about the subject of Dr. Johnson had not he been well documented by Boswell. One of the interesting questions of today, or any day, is: "What was Boswell's first name?"

EXCERPTS FROM LAST "IDLER" ESSAY
"There are few things, not purely evil, of which we can say, without some emotion of uneasiness, this is the last. Those who never could agree together shed tears when mutual discontent has determined them to final separation; of a place which has been frequently visited, though without pleasure, the last look is taken with heaviness of heart; and the Idler, with all his chilliness of tranquility, is not wholly unaffected by the thought that his last essay is before him.

"The secret horror of the last is inseparable from a thinking being, whose life is limited, and to whom death is dreadful. We always make a secret comparison between a part and the whole; the termination of any period of life reminds us that life itself has likewise its termination; when we have done anything for the last time we involuntarily reflect that a part of the days allotted to us is past, and that as more is past there is less remaining."

DR. SAMUEL JOHNSON

SEPTEMBER 21

Summer ends now; now barbarous in beauty the stooks arise
  Around; up above, what wind-walks! what lovely behavior
  of silk-sack clouds! Has wilder, willful-wavier
Meal-drift molded ever and melted across skies?

G.M. HOPKINS
from *Hurrahing in Harvest*

SEPTEMBER 26

Robert Browning and Elizabeth Barrett, or perhaps we'd better say Elizabeth Barrett and Robert Browning, were married on September 26th. It is hard to imagine a more famous literary twosome.

SUMMUM BONUM

All the breath and the bloom of the year in the bag of one bee:
All the wonder and wealth of the mine in the heart of one gem:
In the core of one pearl all the shade and the shine of the sea:
Breath and bloom, shade and shine,—wonder, wealth, and how
Far above them—
  Truth, that's brighter than gem,
  Trust, that's purer than pearl,—
Brightest truth, purest trust in the universe—all were for me
  In the kiss of one girl.

ROBERT BROWNING

Other literary couples that come to mind are Percy and Mary Shelley; Mary may be one of the great unsung writers of our time, since she is the original author of "Frankenstein."

William Sidney Porter, better known as O'Henry, was born in September, 1862.

We celebrate the fact that the Star Spangled Banner was written in September, 1814; that Washington gave his Farewell Address in September, 1796; and William the Conqueror, dissatisfied no doubt with the troubles in Normandy, set off for England with a group of his staunch friends in September, 1066, to see a bit of the country.

A Harvest Moon
A harvest moon!
And on the mats—
Shadows of pine bough.
    KIKATU

OCTOBER 3

ON THE GRASSHOPPER AND THE CRICKET

The poetry of earth is never dead:
When all the birds are faint with the hot sun
And hide in cooling trees, a voice will run
From hedge to hedge about the new-mown mead.
That is the grasshopper's—he takes the lead
In summer luxury,—he has never done
With his delights; for, when tired out with fun,
He rests at ease beneath some pleasant weed.

The poetry of earth is ceasing never.
On a lone winter evening, when the frost
Has wrought a silence, from the stove there shrills
The cricket's song, in warmth increasing ever,
And seems, to one in drowsiness half lost,
The grasshopper's among some grassy hills.
    JOHN KEATS

THE SHEPHERD

How sweet is the shepherd's sweet lot!
From the morn to the evening he strays;
He shall follow his sheep all the day,
And his tongue shall be filled with praise.

For he hears the lamb's innocent call,
And he hears the ewe's tender reply;
He is watchful while they are in peace,
For they know when their shepherd is nigh.
    WILLIAM BLAKE

He that gathereth in summer is a wise son; but he that sleepeth
in harvest is a son that causeth shame.   PROVERBS 10:5

haRvest

As snow in summer, and as rain in harvest, so honour is not seemly for a fool.   PROVERBS 26:1

As the cold of snow in the time of harvest, so is a faithful messenger to them that send him: for he refresheth the soul of his masters.   PROVERBS 25:13

For the Lord said unto me, I will take my rest, and I will consider in my dwelling place like a clear heat upon herbs, and like a cloud of dew in the heat of harvest.

For afore the harvest, when the bud is perfect, and the sour grape is ripening in the flower, he shall both cut off the sprigs with pruning hooks, and take away and cut down the branches.

They shall be left together unto fowls of the mountains, and to beasts of the earth: and the fowls shall summer upon them, and the beasts shall winter upon them.   ISAIAH 18:4-6

The harvest is past, the summer is ended, and we are not saved.   JEREMIAH 8:20

He that observeth the wind shall not sow; and he that regardeth the clouds shall not reap.

In the morning sow thy seed, and in the evening withhold not thine hand: for thou knowest not whether shall prosper, either this or that, or whether they both shall be alike good.
                                    ECCLESIASTES 11:4,6

October

October was the eighth month of the Roman calendar and its name is derived from the Latin octo, meaning eight. There were many attempts to rename it—Gemanicus, Antoninus, and Herculeus. Though all were unsuccessful in catching on, and "October" it remains.

Perhaps the Anglo-Saxons named it more appropriately— "Winmonath," the month of winemaking, or "Winterfylleth," since they believed winter began with the full moon in October.

BIRDS:

With the first snow, tiny kinglets and thrushes head south, along with the last of the warblers, the hawks and shorebirds. V-flocks of Canada geese are on their way south, and this month is the peak of the water-fowl migration, including the woodcock, blue-winged teal, the puddle ducks and diving ducks.

October is the best time to watch for a peregrine falcon on its way to winter residence.

FLOWERS:

Fall foliage is at its peak in New England—sugar maples, dogwood, birch, gingko, beech, sumac, and sourwood have turned all conceivable shades of yellow, orange, red, and purple. The colors of the last remnants of chicory, yarrow, dandelion, hawkeye, and wild asters seem lost in the richer colors of the foliage.

Remove dead wood from trees and shrubs, and prune crowded or crossed branches. Bulbs for crocus, daffodil and tulip should be planted now.

Berries are abundant in October — Hawthorn, holly, dogwood, fire-thorn, bayberry, and black alder provide food for lingering or wintering birds.

TO PRESERVE WILD CRANBERRIES:

Wash the berries several times in cold water. Pack them in sterilized jars and keep them in the refrigerator. They will keep for months.

MAKING WILD GRAPE JELLY:

Wash, stem, and crush both ripe and unripe grapes. Add ¼ cup of water for every quart of grapes and boil for 15 minutes in a covered pot. Strain the juice into a mixing bowl and allow it to sit overnight. During this time the tartrate will crystallize and settle to the bottom.

The next day, without disturbing the crystallized tartrate, dip out the juice into a pot. For every quart of juice add 4 cups of sugar. Boil the juice and sugar mixture until the jelling point is reached (do a jelly test*). Pour the mixture into the jars and seal immediately.

*Jelly test — *Place a small amount of the mixture in a spoon and cool slightly. Let the mixture drop back into the pot from the side of the spoon. If 2 large drops form along the edge of the spoon and come together as one drop, it has reached the jelling point.*

Going to college for me was beyond a doubt the most exciting adventure of my young life. At the last moment some financial arrangements were made and I found myself at a dandy little coeducational college in the middle of Pennsylvania.

It was everything that I hoped it would be (just like in the movies and even more). The world was my oyster. I was in college and I loved it. Then came the great deflator.

An earlier entry in this journal notes the events that took place on the morning of fraternity Rush Week. I'm happy to report that my card, like the dance program of a debutante, did finally get filled and I did go to all of the fraternities and they did take me to lunch and dinner and tried to convince me that they were my kind of fellows and that I was their kind of fellow.

The arrangement was that on a Friday night each of the freshmen who desired to join a fraternity would make a list of the fraternities of his choice, in order, and each of the fraternities would make a list of the freshmen they wished to bid. These were taken to a faculty office and matched up, and then the first dinner would be held that evening amidst candlelight and abracadabra, the freshmen would become Pledges.

Well, I made my choices and then went back up to my room as so instructed to await another portentous knock on the door and a message that would tell me which fraternity I would be joining.

The magic hour was five o'clock. We had been waiting since four-thirty, arrayed with coats and ties. Every moment or so a pair of feet would climb to the fourth floor and would echo down the hall. Then, a knock on the door, a mumbled word of welcome, and 'midst camaraderie and good fellowship, the prospective pledge would be escorted by the brothers to the fraternity house. Many were the footsteps that came down to my end of the hallway, but none stopped in front of my door.

Finally, at five-twenty, there was a knock on the door and once again my roommate and I opened it together. There he stood once again, the big man on the campus, his hand thrust out before him saying: "Welcome." He looked right past me and grabbed my roommate's arm. The two of them soon went downstairs leaving me the only freshman on the fourth floor.

At quarter of six I knew the bell would not toll for me, so I put on my coat, walked down the four flights of stairs and over to the boarding house where I had been taking my meals. I was besieged by youthful doubts—where did I go wrong, perhaps I had been too brash, perhaps I'd been too much of an upstart. There would be no fraternity songs for me, no flickering fireplaces, none of the Christmas dances that I was so assurred were filled with glamour and joy.

At my boarding house I found fifteen other freshman who had failed to make the cut. It turned out to be a beautiful evening.

OCTOBER 8
"Thanks be to God," says the Admiral (Columbus), "the air is soft as in April in Seville, and it is a pleasure to be in it, so fragrant it is."

CHRISTOPHER COLUMBUS Oct. 8, 1492
from Journal of the First Voyage

OCTOBER 10

INDIAN SUMMER

These are the days when birds come back,
A very few, a bird or two,
To take a backward   look.

These are the days when skies put on
The old, old sophistries of June,—
A blue and gold mistake.

Oh, fraud that cannot cheat the bee,
Almost thy plausibility
Induces my belief,

Till ranks of seeds their whiteness bear,
And softly through the altered air
Hurries a timid leaf!

Oh, sacrament of summer days,
Permit a child to join,

Thy sacred emblems to partake,
Thy consecrated bread to break,
Taste thine immortal wine!

EMILY DICKINSON

OCTOBER 14

> From *CHANSON d'AUTOMNE*
> *The long sobbings*
> *Of the violins*
> *Of Autumn*
> *Wound my heart*
> *With monotonous*
> *Languor.*
> PAUL VERLAINE

OCTOBER 25

October, it develops, is a very portentous month in which we celebrate the birth of William Penn in 1644, Alfred Nobel, originator of the prize of the same name, in 1833, Theodore Roosevelt in 1858, dedication of the Statue of Liberty in 1886, and Mohanndas Ghandi in 1869.

There is little commemoration of the famous Black Friday in 1929 which kicked-off the Great Depression.

OCTOBER 28

Today is St. Crispin's Day. The exploits of the original martyrs have been forgotten but Shakespeare in his memorable exhortation of Henry V has forever immortalized this day in literary history. The scene is the Battle of Agincourt. It is Act IV, Scene 3, and Westmoreland has just lamented that there were many soldiers in England that would be useful on the battlefield. Henry replies:

> *Oh, do not wish one more!*
> *Rather proclaim it, Westmoreland, through my host,*
> *That he which hath no stomach to this fight,*
> *Let him depart. His passport shall be made*
> *And crowns for convoy put into his purse.*
> *We would not die in that man's company*
> *That fears his fellowship to die with us.*
> *This day is call'd the feast of Crispian.*
> *He that outlives this day and comes safe home*
> *Will stand a-tiptoe when this day is named*
> *And rouse him at the name of Crispian.*
> *He that shall live this day and see old age*
> *Will yearly on the vigil feast his neighbors*
> *And say, "Tomorrow is Saint Crispian."*
> *Then will he strip his sleeve and show his scars,*
> *And say, "These wounds I had on Crispin's Day."*
> *Old men forget, yet all shall be forgot,*
> *But he'll remember with advantages*

What feats he did that day. Then shall our names,
Familiar in his mouth as household words,
Harry the King, Bedford, and Exeter,
Warwick and Talbot, Salisbury and Gloucester,
Be in their flowing cups freshly remembered.
This story shall the good man teach his son,
And Crispin Crispian shall ne'er go by,
From this day to the ending of the world,
But we in it shall be remembered—
We few, we happy few, we band of brothers.
For he today that sheds his blood with me
Shall be my brother. Be he ne'er so vile,
This day shall gentle his condition.
And gentlemen in England now abed
Shall think themselves accursed they were not here,
And hold their manhoods cheap while any speaks
That fought with us upon Saint Crispin's Day.

OCTOBER 31

John Keats was born this day in 1795. Oddly enough at
school he learned a little Latin but not a syllable of Greek so
that it was very odd that his first sonnet should be entitled: "On
First Looking Into Chapman's Homer."

> *Then I felt like some watcher of the skies*
> *When a new planet swims into his ken;*
> *Or like stout Cortez when with eagle eyes*
> *He stared at the Pacific—and all his men*
> *Looked at each other with a wild surmise—*
> *Silent, upon a peak in Darien.*

Obviously someone must have translated. After a few years
and the appearance of his first successful volume of verse, he
fell in love with one Fanny Brawne (possibly born 100 years too
soon for womens lib), a charming, gay, young, volatile creature
who was something of a flirt. Keats expressed his frustration in
the following lines:

> *Ah! if you prize my subdued soul above*
> *The poor, the fading, brief pride of an hour,*
> *Let none profane my Holy See of love,*
>   *Or with a rude hand break*
>   *The sacramental cake—*
> *Let none else touch the just new-budded flower.*
>   *If not, may my eyes close,*
>   *Love! on their last repose.*

Oscar Wilde

OCTOBER 16

Do you know all those clever things that we've all been saying for years that we think are so original? Actually a great many of them were said first by that tempestuous, controversial master of the turned phrase, Oscar Wilde. He was born on the 16th of October, 1854 in Dublin and always will remain an individual of tremendous singularity. Below is a list of some of those clever one-liners that we think are so original, but that he said first. They are quotations from his plays, letters or from his conversation.

"Men may become old, they never become good."

"He has one of those terribly weak natures that are not susceptible to influence."

"Rich bachelors should be heavily taxed, it is not fair that some men should be happier than others."

"One should never trust a woman who tells one her real age. A woman who would tell one that would tell one anything."

"Women are meant to be loved, not to be understood."

"Every woman is a rebel, and usually in wild revolt against herself."

"She looks like a woman with a past. Most pretty women do."

"The world is a stage, but the play is badly cast."

"Romantic surroundings are the worst surroundings possible for a romantic writer."

"Men marry because they are tired; women because they are curious; both are disappointed."

"Polygamy—how much more poetic it is to marry one and love many."

"To love one's self is the beginning of a life long romance."

"Who, being loved, is poor."

"Washington, D.C. has too many bronzed generals."

"All Americans lecture—I suppose it is something in their climate."

"Niagara Falls—simply a vast unnecessary amount of water going the wrong way and then falling over unnecessary rocks. Every American bride is taken there and the sight of the tremendous waterfall must be one of the earliest if not the keenest disappointments in American married life."

TIPS
ON TRAVELING
TO ENGLAND

Not long ago I made my first trip to the United Kingdom. It was a marvelous adventure from start to finish, but for those of our gentle readers who have never made the trip, I am going to list a few things that I am sure will help to make your trip less confusing and more enjoyable.

1. You will need a passport. To obtain it you will need your birth certificate with the first and last name of your father and mother.

2. There is five hours difference between New York and London. When it is 12 noon in London, it is 7 A.M. on the same day in New York.

3. British money. Basically, the unit is a pound, and there are 100 British pennies (pps) in a pound. With the fluctuating rate of exchange, consider 1 English pound equal to about two and a half American dollars. By all means, get your American money changed into English pounds. At the London Airport, Barclay's Bank maintains a money exchange service.

4. I found the climate a great deal like Seattle, Washington, which means it is a bit warm and dampish and it is a good idea to have a raincoat with you at all times.

5. In London purchase a map of London streets (carry it everywhere and don't be afraid to ask questions.) Also, a map of the London Underground. It takes you to most places and it is fast, safe and well ventilated. The seats, believe it or not, are upholstered with arm rests between each seat.

6. You will be driving on the left hand side of the narrow roads, and you'll find the English drivers are very polite. They generally let you into a line of traffic, at which point you indicate your thanks to them by a thumbs-up sign or the tip of your hat. They do drive fast.

7. English railway systems are a model. The trains run on time, and frequently, and they are clean. You can take a train to most major places in the U.K.

8. London abounds in small hotels that are clean and adequate, and the countryside has literally thousands of pubs, inns and resorts. I'll be reporting upon them in the next edition of "Country Inns and Back Roads."

4. *The Fair of St. Georges Day* by Peter Bruegel, the Elder

EXCVDEBAT

BRVEGEL INVENTOR

November

November was the ninth month of the Roman calendar, and thus its name is from the Latin novem, meaning nine. The Anglo-Saxons gave it a more colorful name however— "Blodmonath"—as a result of the common practice of slaughtering cattle in November for the winter food supply.

BIRDS:

Some vireos, winter wrens, woodcocks, and sparrows may still be lingering behind, however they usually move southward when the food becomes scarce. Northern birds such as brown creepers, snow buntings, nuthatches, juncos, and grosbeaks are arriving from the north. Some of these will continue south; others may remain for the winter.

FLOWERS:

Apply mulch to vegetable gardens and flower beds. Construct protective coverings for shrubs and new trees to avoid damage caused by heavy snow accumulation. It is a good time now to have the lawnmower sharpened and summer tools oiled in preparation for Spring.

This month is your last chance to plant bulbs for Spring flowers or feed and seed the lawn.

REMOVING STAINS:

Alcoholic beverages — Sponge with amyl acetate or cleaning fluid. Wash in hot water and rinse in warm.
Blood — Soak in cold water, then wash in warm water. If the stain still has not come out, soak in a mixture of ammonia and water (2 tbs. ammonia to 1 gallon water).
Chocolate — Soak in cold water and sponge in hot soapy water. Wash in warm or hot water.
Coffee or tea — Pour boiling water through the stain and wash.
Egg — Soak in cold water, then wash in hot water.
Fruits — Rinse in cold running water, then wash in hot water.
Meat, gravy — Soak in cold water and wash in not water.
Milk or cream — Rinse under cold running water and wash in hot water.
Soft drinks — Sponge with lukewarm water and alcohol (equal parts of each), then wash in hot water.

SHAKER BROWN BREAD

1 cup rye flour	
1 cup cornmeal	1¾ cups sour milk
1 cup graham flour	¾ cup molasses
1 teaspoon salt	2 tablespoons butter, melted
¾ teaspoon soda	1 cup chopped raisins

Sift the dry ingredients together and mix well. Combine in a bowl the sour milk, molasses and melted butter. Combine the two mixtures and stir thoroughly, adding the chopped raisins, lightly floured. Pour into two buttered molds. Fill only two-thirds full. Steam for 2 hours and then bake for ½ hour.

NOVEMBER 4

There are probably a few people who note with some interest that today is the birthday of Will Rogers, who was born in 1879. In playing word association games, if one says "Will Rogers" sombody else might say "lasso." It's true that Rogers did appear in the Ziegfield Follies during the 'Teens as a lariat-twirling stand-up comedian, but it was with the advent of radio that he came into his own, and his appearances on Sunday night along with Eddie Cantor at an earlier hour, made the early days of the Great Depression at least bearable.

In some ways he was almost the Mark Twain of his time, except that unlike Twain who could weave an intricate story such as "The Ransom of Red Chief." Rogers best success came with a series of one-liners. His most frequently quoted is: "I never met a man I couldn't like."

NOVEMBER 6

I am not at all certain of the authenticity of this statement but somewhere in the back of my mind November 6th has been set as the day in which Gulliver awakened in Lilliput. I suppose it is as portentous. a day as any. In the "Voyage to Lilliput" we are mirrored as pygmies through the wrong end of the telescope. The affairs of life, with which we seem to be so enthralled, when reduced to a miniature, seem ridiculous and most diminutive. Here is a quotation from a portion of Gulliver's adventures in carrying off the whole fleet of Blefuscu:

> "Lying down behind a hillock, I took out my small perspective glass, and viewed the enemy's fleet at anchor, consisting of about fifty men-o-war, and a great number of transports: I then came back to my house, and gave order (for which I had warrant) for a great quantity of the strongest cable and bars of iron. The cable was about as thick as packthread, and the bars of the length and size of a knitting needle. I trebled the cable to make it stronger, and for the same reason. I twisted three of the iron bars together, binding the extremities into a hook. Having thus fixed fifty hooks to as many cables, I went back to the north-east coast, and putting off my coat, shoes, and stockings, walked into the sea. . . . ."

Jonathan Swift, it appears, was, along with Pope and Homer, one of the first great put-ons of any time.

NOVEMBER 9
ON HIS HAVING ARRIVED AT THE AGE OF TWENTY-THREE

> *How soon hath Time, the subtle thief of youth,*
> *Stolen on his wing my three-and-twentieth year!*
> *My hastening days fly on with full career,*
> *But my late spring no bud or blossom shew'th.*
> *Perhaps my semblance might deceive the truth*
> *That I to manhood am arrived so near;*
> *And inward ripeness doth much less appear,*
> *That some more timely-happy spirits endu'th.*
> *Yet, be it less or more, or soon or slow,*
> *It shall be still in strictest measure even*
> *To that same lot, however mean or high,*
> *Toward which Time leads me, and the will of Heaven.*
> *All is, if I have grace to use it so,*
> *As ever in my great Task-Master's eye.*

JOHN MILTON

NOVEMBER 15

Driving up to Vermont last week, I passed the still smouldering debris of what was obviously a recent barn fire. I've always disliked barn fires. For the first ten years of my life I grew up in a more or less rural atmosphere and when there was a barn fire I always avoided joining the crowds they drew. Somehow the idea of watching the destruction, and worrying about the animals, sent chills through me.

Then there was the night that our barn burned. I loved that barn. It had been some years since it was used for cattle, and the hay in it was at least a dozen years old and, of course, as dry as tinder. But it was everything to the nearby rural kids. We used to make tunnels through the hay and have imaginary wars. We also used it for acrobatic displays, and it was a perpetual stage for plays. By the time we finished jumping and romping in it, the dust from the hay hung over the barn like a London fog, and we would go outside just to get some fresh air. Besides that, the barn had a great barn smell. It was the old wood and the hay and the vestiges of the long departed animals. I can walk into a barn today and be transported immediately back to our barn.

The barn was also the garage for our Summer Car. This was a touring car of the vintage of the early 1920's, and we only ran it after the snow had completely disappeared from the highways.

I don't really know how it all happened, but my mother and I were on the way out of the house one Sunday evening and there were flames coming from one side of the barn. She put her hand over her mouth and said, "Oh, the barn is on fire." I felt a terrible sickening sensation inside. She ran inside and telephoned the local fire department and some of the neighbors came, but we all knew it was to no avail. Soon it was a fiery holocaust, and the barn was providing its own Vikings funeral pyre. The entire structure seemed to be enveloped in flames that rose forty and fifty feet.

Soon the people from all over the neighborhood and the immediate area came to watch our barn burn. They were reassured to know that there were no animals concerned and that nobody was hurt. But it really hurt me to see that some of them could stand around talking normally, maybe even smiling, while our barn was disappearing.

The unkindest cut of all came when the beams, where we had strung many a rope and made many a swing, now let go and came down across the car with a crash. At the same time something within the car's electrical system faulted and the horn began to sound loud and clear, almost as if to say: "If I'm going, I'm going in real style."

I thought that horn would never stop. It sliced into my insides and I began to think about all the rides and all the fun we had enjoyed, and I finally began to cry.

At last the flames subsided and the people began to leave, and we went inside and went to bed and tried to sleep. The next morning I carefully avoided looking at the place where the barn had been. Fortunately, within six weeks we moved away to the big city and I didn't have to look at my friend anymore.

I never go to barn fires.

November 23

In looking over the roster of November events that may have shaken history up a bit, we find the abdication of Kaiser Wilhelm in 1918, the sailing of Magellan around Cape Horn in 1520, and the opening of the Suez Canal in 1869.

On November 19, 1863, Lincoln made his Gettysburg Address, thereby providing schoolboys with meaty rhetoric for the remainder of the ages.

John Milton was born in November, 1608, as well as George Eliot in 1819.

The mention of George Eliot brings to mind that this, of course, is the pen name of Maryanne Evans, who was an immensely popular Victorian novelist who had to write using a male pen name in order to overcome the suppressed women's rights of her times. These suppressed women's rights also make themselves evident in the case of Christina Rossetti, who had to write poetry between getting the housework completed. Emily Dickinson had to bake bread for her household between quatrains.

Pity isn't it, that some of these enlightened souls should have been born into a century where women were third or fourth class citizens? On the other hand, if it weren't for such vigorous spirits as these, perhaps the women of today would not be able to be baseball umpires, jockeys and steeplejacks.

NOVEMBER 24

THREE YOUNG RATS
Three young rats with black felt hats,
Three young ducks with white straw flats,
Three young dogs with curling tails,
Three young cats with demi-veils,
Went out to walk with two young pigs
In satin vests and sorrel wigs;
But suddenly it chanced to rain,
And so they all went home again.
ANONYMOUS

NOVEMBER 25

Intensity was more usually reached by way of the solemn than by way of the brilliant, and such intensity was often arrived at during winter darkness, tempests, and mists. Then Egdon Heath was aroused to reciprocity; for the storm was its lover, and the wind its friend. Then it became the home of strange phantoms; and it was found to be the hitherto unrecognized original of those wild regions of obscurity which are vaguely felt to be compassing us about in midnight dreams of flight and disaster, and are never thought of after the dream till revived by a scene like this.

It was at present perfectly accordant with man's nature — neither ghastly, hateful, nor ugly: neither commonplace, unmeaning, nor tame; but, like man, slighted and enduring; and withal singularly colossal and mysterious in its swarthy monotony.

THOMAS HARDY
From *Return of the Native* Ch. 1

BUNDLING

As the chilly winds of November blow down from the north, we're reminded that the next step for the loving couple in our old engraving might well be to bundle. Much has been made out of this ancient practice which in fact was born out of necessity. More prevalent during the cold months, it conserved the fuel needed for light and heat. The couple went to bed (with proper safeguards) with their clothes on, where they were warm and could talk and woo until late hours. To decrease temptation between bundlers, a low board or bolster divided the bed, or the bundlers wore special garments such as secured nightgowns or bundling bags.

In 1708, Sewal's "Large Dictionary English and Dutch" defined *bundling* as "An odd way of wooing. . . when the wench is gone to bed, the fellow enters the room and lays himself down, in his clothes upon the blanket, next to her, and thus he talks with her very innocently as it is reported." This curious form of courtship was probably brought from the Old World to the New. In America it was practiced by the early rural settlers in New England, as well as by the Dutch and German settlers in Pennsylvania. It was not only a courtship custom, however, but also a gesture of hospitality to travelers. Because of the scarcity of beds, husbands and parents often allowed the traveler to bundle with their wives and daughters.

In Norway the practice of bundling is called "night-running." In Germany it is "going windowing," and in Scotland it is "hand-fasting."

In the Bible, Ruth and Boaz may be considered bundlers—"Tarry this night. . . lie down until morning. And she lay at his feet until morning; and she rose up before one could know another."

In the Middle Ages, bundling was a means by which people tested the power of their moral codes under the extremely tempting conditions of bundling.

In the early days of America, bundling was not considered immoral, and few people, including the clergy, disputed the practice.

It wasn't until after the French and Indian War that the custom of bundling was attacked by the clergymen. "The Pursuit of Happiness" was a play which was concerned with the custom of bundling during the Revolutionary War.

However, bundling fell into disfavor toward the end of the Revolutionary period and became the object of satire and disdain. Anti-bundling songs and poems were widely publicized. Here's one:

> 'Tis not amiss to court and kiss,
> Nor friendship do we blame,
> But bundling in, women with men,
> Upon the bed of shame; . . . .

So today, bundling is for the most part a countryman's joke. Some of the cloistered religious sects such as the Amish still allow it, but can you imagine suggesting bundling to college students in these days of co-ed dorms and twenty-four hour parietel hours?

December

    December derives its name from the Latin word for ten, decem, because it was the tenth month of the Roman calendar. Commodus tried to rename it Amazonius in honor of his hefty mistress, though this name did not catch on.

    It is traditionally a month of rejoicing because the solstice is the beginning of longer periods of daylight in the Northern Hemisphere. Saturnalia and Yule are among the many celebrations which may have influenced the assignation of Christmas to this month.

Wintering birds feed off seeds, berries, and hibernating insects, although bluejays, grosbeaks, chickadees, and winter finches are frequent visitors at your feeder. Such game birds as wild turkeys, pheasant, quail, and ruffed grouse can often be seen in the woodlands. Horned lark, crossbills, and wintering mockingbirds may also have remained behind for Christmas in New England.

FLOWERS:
Witch hazel, Christmas rose, Christmas fern, and club mosses are active in December.

Indoors, kalanchoes and Christmas cacti will flower in December if they are kept in complete darkness from sunset to sunrise beginning in October. A cool temperature and no artificial light after sundown will insure blossoms by Christmastime.

OLD-FASHIONED POTATO SOUP

4 pounds small potatoes	2 quarts milk
2 tablespoons caraway seed	2 tablespoons marjoram, chopped
2 teaspoons salt	
2 quarts water	1 teaspoon paprika
6 small leeks, chopped	6 strips crisp bacon, minced

Scrub the potatoes thoroughly. Do not peel but place in soup pot whole with caraway seed, salt and water. Cook for half an hour, very slowly. Peel potatoes and cut fine; put back into pot with liquor in which they were cooked (the peelings add greatly to the flavor and nourishment.) Add the leeks, top and all, cut fine. Cook for half an hour and pass through coarse sieve. Add milk. Heat well. Add marjoram, paprika and more salt, if necessary. Garnish with minced crisp bacon. Serve with toasted crackers. Serves 8.

KENTUCKY SHOO FLY PIE

¾ cup dark molasses	
¾ cup very hot water	½ cup sugar, brown or maple
½ teaspoon soda	¼ cup butter
1½ cups flour	Pastry for 1 crust

Mix molasses with hot water and blend well. Blend flour, sugar and soda and cut in butter to a coarse crumb. Line pie dish with pastry. Pour in 1/3 of molasses mixture and top with 1/3 crumb mixture. Repeat adding alternate layers with crumb on top. Bake for about 35 minutes at 375 degrees.

DECEMBER 3

Last night at my neighbor's house a group of us played a sort of non-game in which we would choose one person, living or dead, with whom we would prefer to spend thirty days in a semi-private hospital room. The ground rules also were explicit on the subject that both parties were positively bedridden and there was to be no hanky-panky.

I was surprised at some of the answers. In fact I was sorry I didn't think of some of them myself. One girl said that she thought that Oscar Wilde would prove to be the most amusing man with whom to spend thirty days under such conditions, and when it came down to amusement someone else immediately chimed in with Noel Coward. One of the men chose Winston Churchill's mother, based he said on the recent book about her. Of course, there were such entries as Albert Schweitzer, Napoleon, (although everyone agreed that his ego trip couldn't include anybody else.) Abraham Lincoln and Philip of Macedon.

The more we talked the longer the list of candidates became and everyone became tremendously stimulated to look up names in the Oxford Book of English and American Literature.

DECEMBER 5

A BIRTHDAY

My heart is like a singing bird
   Whose nest is in a watered shoot;
My heart is like an apple-tree
   Whose boughs are bent with thick-set fruit;
My heart is like a rainbow shell
   That paddles in a halcyon sea;
My heart is gladder than all these,
   Because my love is come to me.
Raise me a dais of silk and down;
   Hang it with vair and purple dyes;
Carve in it doves and pomegranates,
   And peacocks with a hundred eyes;
Work it in gold and silver grapes,
   In leaves and silver fleur-de-lys;
Because the birthday of my life
   Is come, my love to me.

CHRISTINA ROSSETTI
Dec. 5, 1830

DECEMBER 12

WRITTEN AT AN INN AT HENLEY

To thee, fair freedom! I retire
    From flattery, cards, and dice, and din;
Nor art thou found in mansions higher
    Than the low cot or humble inn.

'Tis here with boundless power I reign;
    And every health which I begin
Converts dull port to bright champagne;
    Such freedom crowns it, at an inn.

I fly from pomp, I fly from plate!
I fly from falsehood's specious grin!
Freedom I love, and form I hate,
    And choose my lodgings at an inn.

Here, waiter! take my sordid ore,
    Which lacqueys else might hope to win;
It buys, what courts have not in store,
    It buys me freedom at an inn.

Whoe'er has traveled life's dull round,
    Where'er his stages may have been,
May sigh to think he still has found
    The warmest welcome at an inn.

WILLIAM SHENSTONE

DECEMBER 20

Elsewhere in this journal it is recorded that at the time I was 4 years old, after running riot over a series of nursemaids and elderly ladies who were hired by the score by my widowed father to look after me during the daytime, he wooed and married a very remarkable lady whom I have always referred to as "mother."

They were married in September, and for some reason that I have never thoroughly understood, the prospect of spending their first Christmas along with an incorrigible child was a prospect that thrilled my new mother right down to the tips of her size 6B shoes. She and my father spent weeks of whispered consultations about what exactly would be done for this special Christmas. I was thoroughly indoctrinated in the Santa Claus legend, and for a week before Christmas they started explaining patiently to me that Santa Claus would arrive on Christmas Eve and that if I was a good little fellow he might leave a few things

under the tree, and that we would all go down early on Christmas morning and see all the presents. I, of course, was absolutely beside myself with greed and anticipation.

Finally came the Night Before Christmas.

It can be recorded now that my father stayed up until at least 3
A.M. trying to get the electric train set to work. A friend of
his passing by happened to see the lights on in the living room
and came in. In 48 seconds he found the break in the track
and the American Flyer was tooting merrily around the tree
and into the corners, as well.

At long last, Dad and Mother stood gazing at the tree sat-
isfied that there wasn't a single thing out of place. Every orna-
ment had been created for every single niche, every bulb was
busy creating a Christmas glow second to none, and the tree's
symmetry was a thing of beauty.

So hand in hand, their first Christmas together, they went
up the stairway, peeked in at my room where I was angelically
asleep, placed a present at the foot of my bed. It had been
explained to me very carefully that Santa would leave one

thing for me which I could open and then wait until they came in in the morning and we could all go downstairs together.

And so, blessed calm finally descended upon the household. That is, until the first faint streaks of dawn invaded the window of the sleeping babe, and I awakened, fully aware of where I was and what day it was.

My grubby little fingers tore open a carefully wrapped package and there I found a stuffed squirrel with a very bushy tail, which I might add is still among my collection of memorabilia. I gurgled at it, pushed it, pulled it, yanked at the tail, and tried to remove its little green coat, which was fortunately sewed on by tough-fingered peasants from Czechoslovakia. I became bored.

My eyes cast about the room for some other means of entertainment and then I remembered the Christmas tree downstairs. All thoughts, all admonitions of remaining in my own bedroom until summoned, immediately left.

I opened the door cautiously, looked craftily into the hall to see if the coast was clear. It was. So, downstairs I crept like the felon I was, and there in the living room glistening and heavy laden was the Tree. Underneath the tree were the Presents. Santa had arrived!

A warning system of some kind must have been operating in my brain because I did not open any of the presents. Instead, my eye caught a small violin nestling in the branches of the tree about an inch out of my reach. I moved closer to the tree. I stretched. It was still out of reach. I backed away and looked around for a chair upon which I might stand. Apparently there was none available. I moved back directly under the violin once more. I stood on my tippy toes. No. I took three steps backward and let go with a running jump. Fagin, himself, could not have felt such penultimate joy as when my claw-like fingers grasped the long neck of this violin and I jerked it away from the tree. However, the Worst was yet to come, for the violin had been wired to the tree and as I grabbed it, it pulled the tree over. I watched with horror as down it came, with what I am sure was the loudest and most resounding crash ever heard on Christmas morn.

The ornaments were shattered, the electricity shorted, the trunk came down over four boxes containing presents—it was an absolutely Instant Catastrophe.

True to my code, I turned tail, ran upstairs into my room, burrowed under the covers and was the picture of sweet innocence if ever there was one. It was a world record for the twenty-five yard dash that has never been bettered.

The sound, of course, brought both my father and his new spouse bolt upright in bed. They heard the scampering of feet, and with some misgiving, went downstairs to view the scene.

My mother reported in later years, that while she laughed hysterically my father saw nothing funny or humorous, and in fact sat down on the floor and wept openly.

And what would you have done if you were the parents of such a culprit and it being Christmas morning? You can hardly beat a kid on Christmas Day. So, I was instructed to remain in bed all day with no presents.

About two o'clock in the afternoon when my mother's sisters and their husbands began to arrive from the country, I was absolutely beside myself. I could hear them all below stairs having a good time, and I failed to understand why as each new aunt and uncle arrived it was soon followed by loud guffaws of laughter.

Pretty soon they all began to creep upstairs one at a time, each with some present for me. Soon my bed and the area around it was surrounded with wrapping paper and open boxes. My uncle George, with a twinkle in his eye, brought the most portentous of them all—the violin.

Turned out to be some kind of Christmas.

GHOSTS OF CHRISTMAS PAST

We are, of course, indebted to Charles Dickens for the title of this section, in fact we are indebted to Dickens for a great many of the emotional tugs of Christmas. Certainly his "A Christmas Carol" is rich in references and ideas that make the spirit of Christmas much more vivid.

Many interesting scheduled and unscheduled events have taken place during the Christmas seasons of the past. It is obvious from the list that some of the participants were aware of the great propaganda value of creating events that would, by-a-not-so-odd-coincidence, fall on Christmas Day. Here are a few:

In 486 A.D., in order to win support of the more powerful bishops, Clovis, the king of the Franks, was baptized.

In 800 A.D. Charlemagne was crowned Holy Roman Emperor.

In 1066 William the Conqueror was crowned King of England in Westminster Abbey.

In 1190 Richard the Lionhearted held a grand banquet during which some of his allies started to brawl.

In 1492 Christopher Columbus was sailing along the coast of Hispaniol in search of natives to barter gold. The "Santa Maria" ran aground and he spent Christmas Day unloading her in an attempt to refloat her.

In 1620 while still living on board the Mayflower, the Pilgrims began to build their Common House on Christmas Day.

In 1642 Sir Isaac Newton was born on Christmas Day.

On Christmas Day in 1645 riots broke out in England in protest against the Puritanical decree that Christmas Day be spent in fasting and penitence.

On Christmas Eve in 1776 George Washington and his men crossed the Delaware and surprised the British and Hessian soldiers who were tipsy from their Christmas celebrations.

In 1864 General Sherman sent President Lincoln a telegram saying: "I beg to present you as a Christmas gift the city of Savannah."

On Christmas Day in 1875 Boss Tweed of New York's Tammany Hall hid on a New Jersey farm after escaping from jail.

In 1968, the Apollo 8 astronauts fired their main engine and headed for home on Christmas Eve.

A common dish on Queen Elizabeth's table at Christmas was a monster pie from which a number of birds flew when it was opened.

The Duke of Buckingham entertained Queen Henrietta, the wife of Charles the First of England, one Christmas; he served a pie from which a tiny dwarf dressed as Santa Claus appeared when the crust was removed.

In 1769 a Christmas pie was made for Sir Henry Gray. It was 9 feet in circumference and weighed 200 pounds. It was composed of 2 bushels of flour, 20 lbs. of butter, 4 geese, 2 turkeys, 2 rabbits, 2 wild ducks, 2 woodcock, 6 snipe, 2 curlews, 2 neats' tongues, 4 partridges, 7 blackbirds, and 7 pigeons.